Georgia Wetlands

Trends and Policy Options

Georgia Wetlands

Trends and Policy Options

by James E. Kundell
and S. Wesley Woolf

Carl Vinson Institute of Government
The University of Georgia

GEORGIA WETLANDS: TRENDS AND POLICY OPTIONS

Editing: John Gaither, Inge Whittle
Design and production: Reid McCallister
Production assistant: Mary Porter
Typesetting: Anne Huddleston
Proofreading: Susan McLain
Publications editor: Emily Honigberg

Figures 2, 3, 7, 8, 9, 10 by Nanette Manhart.
Cover photo courtesy of Georgia Department of Industry and Trade.

Library of Congress Cataloging-in-Publication Data

Kundell, James E.
  Georgia Wetlands.

  Bibliography: p.
  1. Wetland conservation—Georgia. 2. Wetlands—Georgia. 3. Environmental policy—Georgia. I. Woolf, S. Wesley. II. Title
QH76.5.G4K86   1986   333.91'8'09758   86-18956
ISBN 0-89854-116-6

Foreword

Georgia is experiencing Sunbelt population growth and expansion in agricultural and forestry activities resulting in increased pressure to convert wetlands to other uses. The state provided protection to coastal wetlands with the passage of the Marshlands Protection Act of 1970, but no such protection has been afforded freshwater wetlands in Georgia. Since wetlands provide a variety of goods and services to the state, a study was undertaken to determine the current state of wetlands, what problems are evident, and what alternatives are available to address these problems.

The research on which this publication is based was financed in part by the U.S. Department of the Interior, as authorized by the Water Research and Development Act of 1978 (P.L. 95-467), and presented in the research report, *Analysis of Wetland Trends and Management Alternatives for Georgia*. This publication expands upon the research report and presents the policy options related to wetlands in Georgia.

The authors of this work are Dr. James E. Kundell, senior associate, and Mr. S. Wesley Woolf, research specialist, in the Governmental Research and Services Division of the Carl Vinson Institute of Government.

Melvin B. Hill, Jr.
Director

Contents

7 **Conclusions** **94**

FIGURES

TABLES

1 Introduction

Georgia has an extensive belt of coastal saltwater marshlands that separate the coastal barrier islands from the mainland of Georgia. Characterized as the "Marshes of Glynn" by Georgia's poet laureate Sidney Lanier, the salt marshes are an integral part of coastal Georgia and are accepted as a familiar segment of the landscape. Awareness of the values inherent to saltwater marshes, especially those values essential to the coastal fishing industry, culminated in legislative action providing for orderly development in coastal Georgia that might otherwise alter these sensitive environments. In the process, public attention became focused on these very economically and ecologically productive natural systems.

Inland freshwater wetlands are much more extensive and variable than coastal marshes, but less attention has been paid to these areas. In recent years evidence has accumulated indicating a wide range of beneficial functions performed by freshwater wetlands and the types of problems that may result from their alteration. This, in turn, has stimulated consideration of legislative and other mechanisms to ensure that freshwater wetlands are not needlessly converted to other uses.

This book is designed to present an overview of the wetland situation in Georgia. Consideration is given to the nature and extent of wetlands, particularly freshwater wetlands, in the state. The salt marshes in the state are geographically more compact and are better understood, better mapped, and better protected than freshwater wetlands. Freshwater wetlands, however, provide a wide variety of benefits related to environmental quality, fish and wildlife habitat, and socioeconomic functions such as flood protection.

Georgia has more wetland acreage than most other states. A number of studies have been conducted in the state and nationally to quantify wetland acreage. Studies which provide the best insights into the wetland situation in Georgia include those conducted by the Georgia Department of Natural Resources, the U.S. Fish and Wildlife Service, and the USDA Soil Conservation

Service. The most recent analysis conducted by the Fish and Wildlife Service compared quantified wetland acreage in the mid-1950s to recently quantified wetland acreage for the mid-1970s, indicating the rate of wetland conversion in the state. As wetlands are filled, drained, or in other ways converted to dryland uses, the values associated with these wetlands are irretrievably lost.

Steps have been taken at numerous levels of government to provide wetlands with some form of protection from conversion. Federal wetland protection efforts are authorized by Section 404 of the Clean Water Act. The federal wetlands program, however, is limited in both the types of wetlands and the types of activities included. Thus, several states have implemented wetland protection measures either by enacting specific wetland protection legislation or by adapting other laws to afford protection to wetlands. Some of these state approaches allow for local governments to implement the program. Many local governments also have wetland protection authority under their state-granted ''home rule'' powers.

Because efforts to properly manage wetland environments may conflict with the rights of private property owners, the courts have often been summoned to resolve disputes over wetland areas. A review of the accumulated case law brings to light the degree of wetland protection allowed under state and local government police powers to protect the health, safety, and welfare of the public. Further protection is often afforded through outright public and private purchase or through mechanisms for compensating private wetland owners for their loss.

Consideration of the wetland situation in Georgia requires the intertwining of forces and events evident in Georgia with those acting at the national level. Our understanding of wetland values and our attitudes toward these wetlands are meshed with those of other states and regions. To develop an adequate perspective of Georgia's wetland resource, let us first consider what wetlands are, the values associated with these wetlands, and the forces involved in their conversion to dryland uses. By so doing, we may better perceive the costs and benefits involved in wetland conversions and to whom these costs and benefits accrue.

2 Perspective

To present an overview of the wetland situation in Georgia, we must first examine the overall national wetland trends and the results of research and management efforts in other regions of the country.

TYPES OF WETLANDS

Wetlands include various types of marshes, swamps, bogs, and bottomlands—lands periodically or continually inundated by water. They are found along sloping areas between upland and deepwater environments or in basins isolated from other surface waters. Where a wetland begins or ends in this continuum or transition zone between land and water is not always easily identified.

Factors Determining and Delimiting Wetlands

The characteristics principally relied upon to define and delimit wetlands are hydrology, vegetation, and soils. Approaches vary among federal and state agencies as to how these factors should be employed to determine the wetland borders.

Hydrology

Wetlands are of two basic hydrologic types. For one type, water flows through the wetland that is located between an upland area and another body of water. It thus serves as a transition zone between the terrestrial and aquatic environments. Wetlands of this type are frequently associated with ground water seepage and are generally referred to as riverine floodplains, riparian wetlands, river swamps, or bottomland hardwoods. The second type of freshwater wetland tends to be located in isolated basins that have varying sources of water input and frequently have a relatively impermeable soil substrate.

The two most influential hydrologic factors determining the characteristics of freshwater wetlands are the depth of the water and the pattern of water depth fluctuation.[1] Both factors are in turn determined by the local climate and the source of water feeding the wetland.

The average depth of water over time will determine, among other things, the species of plants that can compete most successfully under the specific hydrologic conditions, the rate of decomposition of organic matter, and the types of soils formed in the wetland. As a result, both the vegetative species and soil types associated with wetlands reflect the long-term hydrologic situation.

Average water depth can vary greatly in different wetland types. Some may be saturated only to the soil surface; others may be inundated with several feet of standing water. Deeper wetlands are characterized by open water in which rooted vegetation does not extend above the water level.

Since most plants are adapted to live in a relatively narrow range of water depths, the rate and degree of water level fluctuations can determine which plants will survive in an area. Water depth fluctuations can also determine the rate and degree of mineral and gas exchange and the rate of plant growth. The timing of these fluctuations is also important. While inundating a bottomland hardwood forest during the dormant winter months may have little long-term impact on tree growth, inundation during the growing season may have a significant impact.

Water level fluctuations may occur daily for tidally influenced coastal marshlands or seasonally with respect to riverine floodplains. Isolated basins experience fluctuating water levels with intermittent rainfall.

Vegetation

As previously mentioned, the average water depth and the fluctuation patterns influence the composition of a wetland's vegetative landscape. Water inundation during the growing season can be a major limiting factor for most plants in need of oxygenated root systems. Conversely, winter flooding alone may have little or no effect upon dormant vegetative communities. Vegetation type is the most commonly utilized factor in distinguishing among various wetland environments.

Soils

Until recently, when the U.S. Fish and Wildlife Service (FWS) refined its wetland definition to include soil characteristics,[2] soils were rarely if ever an element considered in delimiting wetland environments. Although direct correlation of soil and wetland types has not proven completely reliable,[3] hydric soils are usefully employed as one factor in the FWS definitional framework, which is being widely accepted as the national standard for identifying wetlands (see Figure 1). A list of hydric soils is currently being developed by the Soil Conservation Service.[4]

Defining Wetlands

Wetlands have been historically defined according to the end sought to be achieved and to some extent still are. Thus definitions varied considerably among waterfowl managers, flood control engineers, water quality experts, and soil scientists. Similarly, definitions vary considerably between federal agencies with different regulatory responsibilities, such as the U.S. Army Corps of Engineers (COE) and the Department of the Interior's Fish and Wildlife Service (FWS).

If any form of management program for freshwater wetlands is to be effective, however, the areas to be covered by that program must be specifically determined. Thus, a working definition of a wetland is essential, as is a method for determining wetland boundaries.

Various systems of defining wetland environments are being employed by different agencies at all levels of government. Federal governmental agencies often utilize very broad systems of identification designed to incorporate all types of wetlands within the United States. The FWS defines wetlands as follows:[5]

> Wetlands are lands transitional between terrestrial and aquatic systems where the water table is usually at or near the surface or the land is covered by shallow water. For purposes of this classification wetlands must have one or more of the following three attributes: (1) at least periodically, the land supports predominantly hydrophytes; (2) the substrate is predominantly undrained hydric soil; and (3) the substrate is nonsoil and is saturated with water or covered by shallow water at some time during the growing season of each year.

This definition requires that a wetland support at least periodically predominantly wetland vegetation; or that the underlying soil be of the type produced by a wetlands environment; or if the wetland is not underlain by soil as might be the case with a limesink, that the bottom be saturated with water or covered with shallow water during part of the growing season. In most cases, a wetland will have all three attributes.

Wetland Types

According to the 1956 FWS analysis, 20 types of wetlands are found in the United States. The 1984 FWS report expands this classification system to include some 55 distinct types within the upper levels of the classification hierarchy. These wetland types are presented in Figure 1.

VALUES OF WETLANDS

Wetland values are not necessarily reflected in the Fish and Wildlife Service definition of wetlands. This is primarily because of variations in the ecological and resource values within any particular wetland type. Understanding wetland values can help in choosing alternatives that make the best use of wetlands at the least cost. Many Georgians, perhaps unknowingly, are better off for having a healthy wetland environment.

Figure 1: *Classification Hierarchy for Wetlands and Deepwater Habitats*

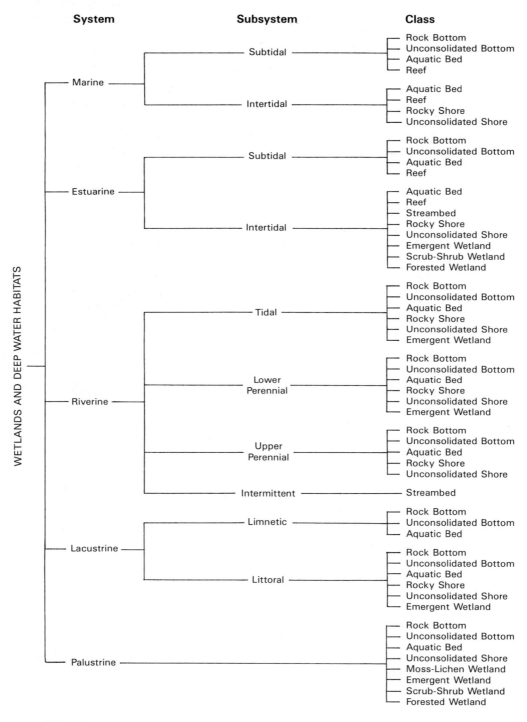

FWS, *Wetlands of the United States: Current Status and Recent Trends,* 1984.

Historically, the values of wetlands have not been well understood. For over a century, wetlands were thought to be sources of pestilence and impediments to development and travel. Congressional action in the mid-nineteenth century and government policy until the mid-twentieth century were significant factors in the drastic wetland losses during that time.

Scientific knowledge has slowly accumulated evidence of the valuable resource potential of many wetland environments. The 1956 FWS inventory of wetlands did much to change attitudes and inform the public of the services performed by wetlands in their natural state. More recently, President Carter conveyed this evolving public understanding in a 1977 environmental message:

> The nation's coastal and inland wetlands are vital natural resources of critical importance to the people of this country. Wetlands are areas of great natural productivity, hydrological utility, and environmental diversity, providing natural flood control, improved water quality, recharge of aquifers, flow stabilization of streams and rivers, and habitat for fish and wildlife resources. Wetlands contribute to the production of agricultural products and timber and provide recreational, scientific, and esthetic resources of national interest.

Increasing knowledge of wetlands' importance for the protection of water quality, game and fish habitat, and for socioeconomic values such as flood protection has sharpened the public appreciation with which wetlands are viewed. Table 1 lists values generally associated with wetlands. Although variation is the rule among individual wetland environments, generally, wetlands are capable of possessing a wide variety of intrinsic ecological and resource values. To better enable researchers and managers to determine the values of wetlands, the FWS is in the process of developing its "National Wetlands Values Bibliographic Data Base," which currently contains some 4,000 research citations related to wetland values.[6]

Discussion of the value of a wetland resource necessarily brings forward questions regarding to whom the value is accruing. Wetlands maintain little value in the competitive markets with which we are familiar, primarily because such values do not accrue to any single market competitor. Rather, the public at large is the benefactor of sound wetlands management practices, primarily in the form of preventive maintenance. That is, wetlands are not generally valued for a product that can be generated, but for public expenditures foregone as a result of a healthy wetland environment. These values are generally referred to as "nonmarket values."

A broad understanding of resource values is necessary if management alternatives are to encompass the wide range of possible public benefits. Wetlands are quite variable in the benefits they bestow upon particular environs, depending on local variations in hydrology, soils, vegetation, and topography. Such highly site-specific characteristics impose difficulties in aligning characteristic wetland types with the values that may or may not be present. As presented in Table 1, this overview can be divided into three basic types of wetland values: (1) environmental quality values, (2) fish and wildlife values, and (3) socio-economic values.

Environmental Quality Values

Maintenance and enhancement of environmental quality is a valuable attribute of wetlands. Water quality improvements and local climatic moderation are two functions performed by wetlands in this regard.

Table 1: *Major Wetland Values*

Environmental Quality Values
Water Quality Maintenance
    Pollution Filter
    Sediment Removal
    Oxygen Production
    Nutrient Recycling
    Chemical and Nutrient Absorption
Aquatic Productivity
Microclimate Regulator
World Climate (Ozone layer)

Fish and Wildlife Values
Fish and Shellfish Habitat
Waterfowl and Other Bird Habitat
Furbearer and Other Wildlife Habitat

Socioeconomic Values
Flood Control
Wave Damage Protection
Erosion Control
Ground Water Recharge and Water Supply
Timber and Other Natural Products
Energy Source (Peat)
Livestock Grazing
Fishing and Shellfishing
Hunting and Trapping
Recreation
Aesthetics
Education and Scientific Research

Adapted from U.S. Fish and Wildlife Service, *Wetlands of the United States: Current Status and Recent Trends,* 1984.

Water Quality Improvement

Wetlands assist in maintaining or improving water quality by intercepting upland runoff and filtering nutrients, wastes, and sediment from waters passing to bodies of deeper water such as rivers. Downstream water quality is improved by temporarily retaining such pollutants so that they are trapped in the wetland sediments or assimilated by the vegetation. Retention of nutrients and other wastes is often accomplished by way of their adsorption to sediment and the settling of that sediment in the wetland. Sediment removal is one of the major functions contributing to downstream water quality.

Trapped nutrients and pollutant wastes can, however, be remobilized by means of plant uptake or subsequent wetland disturbance. Plant uptake can result in consumption by fish or wildlife and consequent bioaccumulations up the food chain. Natural or human-induced wetland disturbances can result in severe releases of toxic substances into the downstream flow. Temporary retention can, however, degrade many wastes into harmless forms or allow a gradual release of toxins or nutrients into downstream systems.

Many proposals have been made for certain types of wetlands to be used to process domestic wastes. Significant improvements in water quality have been achieved in Wisconsin's Brillion Marsh, which has been receiving domestic wastes since 1923.[7] A dramatic example of wetland waste treatment capabilities is Tinicum Marsh, a freshwater tidal marsh near Philadelphia, Pennsylvania. On a daily basis, the marsh was shown to remove 7.7 tons of biological oxygen demand, 4.9 tons of phosphorus, 4.3 tons of ammonia, and 138 lbs. of nitrate from the effluent of three sewage treatment plants. Tinicum Marsh adds 20 tons of oxygen to the water daily.[8] It is estimated, however, that about 250 acres of wetlands are required to assimilate one million gallons of sewage per day.[9] Thus, this approach would most likely be suitable only for smaller communities with limited sewage discharges.

In Georgia, the Alcovy River's bottomland forested wetlands were shown to significantly improve water quality after human and chicken wastes had "grossly polluted" the river three miles upstream. Wharton[10] estimated the water pollution control value of the 2,300 acre swamp at $1 million per year.

Wetlands may also perform similar purification functions with respect to ground water. Those wetlands hydrologically connected to the ground water regime could also be a source of recharge for underground water supplies, in which case the natural settling and filtering of pollutants would preserve the purity of the water resource. Purification of water recharging a ground water resource, particularly in Southwest Georgia's limesink areas, could be essential to maintaining high water quality values necessary for human consumption and industrial growth.

Climatic and Atmospheric Functions

Wetlands are a source of water to the atmosphere and can play a role in local and regional droughts. For instance, Hefner and Brown hypothesized that wetland drainage could reduce wetland thunderstorm activity in Florida.[11] One study of cumulus clouds in Florida found noticeable effects on clouds by lakes more than one mile in diameter.[12]

Local temperatures have shown to be moderated by the presence of wetlands. For example, drained agricultural areas in Florida were found to be five degrees colder in winter than surrounding undrained areas.[13]

Fish and Wildlife Values

Fish and wildlife benefit from the natural functioning of wetland environments in two ways: (1) by the provision of food and habitat, and (2) through food chain support. Food chain support in freshwater wetlands is a consequence of spring flooding and the accompanying influx of nutrient-rich sediments. The effect of such influxes combined with the nutrients already accumulated is a very high rate of plant productivity. The fertility of floodplains resulting from annual flooding and sediment deposition provides a widely recognized example. This is also true in coastal marshes where tidal fluctuations increase productivity, supporting among other things the coastal commercial fisheries.

High levels of plant productivity contribute to corresponding levels of invertebrate organisms upon which fish and other wildlife feed. Most species of freshwater fishes are heavily dependent upon wetland feeding areas or upon wetland-produced food. In addition, almost all recreationally important freshwater fishes use wetlands as nursery and/or spawning grounds.

Southern bottomland hardwood forests serve as nursery and feeding grounds for warmouth and largemouth bass, and their adult counterparts feed and spawn there. The bottomlands of Georgia's Altamaha River are used by hickory shad and blueback herring for spawning.[14] In fact, Wharton[15] concluded that river swamps in Georgia produce about 1,300 pounds of fish per acre yearly.

Likewise, coastal wetlands with very high levels of plant productivity provide nutrients that are flushed into adjacent estuaries. Although the overall importance of coastal plant production to saltwater fishes is unknown, it does contribute to the approximately 4.08 billion pounds of estuarine-dependent fish and shellfish that were landed by U.S. commercial fishermen in 1980. This amounted to 63 percent of U.S. commercial landings at U.S. ports with a dockside value equalling $1.15 billion or 51.5 percent of total catch value.[16]

Plant decomposition in wetlands is also important for waterfowl. Leaf decomposition in bottomland hardwoods is an important source of protein for egg-laying waterfowl.[17] Thus, the natural influx and decomposition of nutrient-rich plant material provides the front-end support of a wetland food chain upon which many commercially and recreationally important fish and wintering water-fowl depend.

Wetlands provide habitat and food sources important to fish and wildlife populations. Because of their high levels of plant productivity, wetlands provide a relatively high carrying capacity for certain wildlife species. For example, bottomland hardwood forests have been found to support twice as many white-tail deer per acre as do upland forests.

Wetlands also contribute to wildlife habitat by providing protective cover of various sorts. Numerous species of birds, mammals, and fish utilize freshwater wetland environments for nesting purposes. Wetland vegetation provides protection from predators during this critical stage of their life cycle. Protection is also provided to less wetland-dependent wildlife during periods of environmental stress, such as upland drought and overwintering. Southeastern and other swamps have been found to provide alternative food sources when upland resources have diminished.

Wetlands provide critical habitat for a number of endangered species of animals and plants. Although wetlands constitute less than 5 percent of the nation's total land area, almost 35 percent of all rare and endangered animals are in some way dependent upon wetland habitat.[18] Many endangered plants are likewise dependent upon wetland environments.

Wildlife resources contribute considerably to the nation's economy. The FWS estimated that 50 percent of all hunters 16 years old or older spent $638 million hunting migratory waterfowl in 1980 alone. More impressive is the estimated $148 billion spent by the same age group on observing and photographing fish and wildlife. Other economic ramifications include the $295 million harvest value of wetland fur-bearing mammals (equal to almost one-third of total harvest value of the U.S. fur industry), the $1.7 million generated from the sale of alligator hides in controlled harvests in Louisiana, and the $11 million of crayfish harvested in Louisiana alone.

Socioeconomic Benefits

The socioeconomic values provided by wetlands include flood protection, erosion control, ground water recharge, and production of harvestable natural products. There are also nonmarket values obtained from wetlands which benefit society.

Flood Protection

The flood protection value of a particular wetland is largely a function of its topography. Topographical depressions and floodplain corridors provide flood-waters storage. Consequently, downstream areas benefit from reductions in both floodpeaks and flooding frequency.

Development in the immediate floodplain or the filling of wetland depressions necessarily conveys the water flow back to the primary flow corridor, thus increasing the quantity and the velocity of downstream flow. Downstream areas will then experience flooding that may destroy public and private property, requiring public remedial expenditures with the simultaneous loss of the taxable property base. Agricultural lands, which in some cases are previously drained wetlands, bear the overwhelming proportion of flood damage acreages in the conterminous United States.

Wetland flood storage values were recognized and acted upon by the U.S. Army Corps of Engineers in Massachusetts. In the early 1970s, the Corps considered several alternatives for providing flood protection in the Charles River basin just upstream from Boston. Rejecting its options to build a large reservoir or to construct extensive walls and dikes, the Corps concluded that the least cost solution was perpetual protection of 8,500 acres of basin wetlands, the loss of which was calculated to cause average annual flood damage of $17 million. In 1983, the Corps completed the acquisition program.

Erosion Control

Freshwater wetlands adjacent to river corridors are especially effective in controlling shoreline soil erosion and intercepting eroded soil from upland areas. Wetland vegetation, in binding sediments via root systems and slowing the velocity of flooding waters, is the primary mechanism by which erodible sediments are retained. Soil erosion also causes the sedimentation of waterways, upon which millions of dollars are spent annually to maintain navigability, and the increased turbidity of waters, of which many will require treatment for municipal water supplies. Coastal estuaries of commercial importance can also be damaged by incoming sediment loads. Thus, erosion and sedimentation can cause an immense drain on public revenues. The effectiveness of wetlands in reducing these erosion and sedimentation impacts has been well documented.

Ground Water Recharge

Some wetlands may recharge ground water supplies by allowing standing water to percolate through the soil to the saturation zone. The amount of recharge from isolated basins will vary depending on the permeability of the underlying soil strata. Ground water recharge may occur[19] in wetlands transitional between upland and lower deepwater environments. Recent research indicates that wetlands may also serve as a discharge point for ground water.[20] Thus, at different times of the year, wetlands may recharge or be recharged by the underlying ground water regime. The interaction between a wetland environment and a ground water resource is vital to a state's public health and economic growth, especially in Georgia where the southern half leans on the economic crutch of a presently plentiful and high quality ground water supply.

The value of any wetland for ground water protection is determined by the surrounding topographic characteristics and by the quality and quantity of the ground water resource it recharges. Upland areas are often the source of ground water recharge rather than the many wetlands underlain by relatively impermeable layers of clay.[21] Likewise, a ground water resource not usable for public water supply because of high mineral or pollutant content or because of a low quantity output may reduce the significance of a wetland's recharge function. Because of the variability in ground water recharge capability and uncertainties in the science of ground water hydrology, any wetland likely to be functioning as a recharge area should be the subject of careful management.

Harvestable Natural Products

Wetlands provide a variety of harvestable natural products including timber, peat, cranberries and blueberries, and wild rice. Grazing of wetland grasses occurs in many areas of the country and haying of such grasses provides winter livestock feed.

Commercial forested wetlands occupy an estimated 82 million acres of wetlands in the 49 continental states.[22] Most of this acreage lies east of the Rockies, the southern wetland forests alone having an $8 billion dollar standing value. These southern forests have been harvested for over 200 years without noticeable degradation; conversion of bottomland hardwoods in the Mississippi Delta to agricultural production, however, has reduced wetlands in this region by 75 percent.[23] Drainage of wetland environments for timber production is occurring throughout the southeastern United States, reducing the influx of waterborne nutrients and, consequently, the productivity of the site.

Peat is another harvestable wetland product used mainly as horticulture in the United States. Europeans have used peat as heating fuel for centuries. Peat mining, however, destroys the wetland and most of its associated values.

Other Values of Wetlands

The quantification of wetland values for societal benefits reflects an attempt to direct the attention of policymakers to some very real benefits provided by wise resource management policies. Wetlands possess values other than those that are tangible and subject to economic quantification, however. These include aesthetics, education, and research.

Aesthetics. Several studies have found that wetlands present a high quality aesthetic natural environment. In fact, of the top 25 national wildlife refuges most visited, 19 have significant wetland components.[24] This represents approximately 50 percent of the total 1981 visitation to all U.S. National Wildlife Refuge units.[25] The Okefenokee Swamp in south Georgia, one of the largest and best preserved freshwater wetlands in the United States, ranked 21st nationally in 1981 visitation, with 257,927 visitors. The interface of land and water and the peculiar adaptations of wetland flora and fauna are particularly appealing to many people.[26]

Education and research. Science education is a major theme at many parks and public areas containing wetlands. Likewise, much scientific research is carried on in wetland environments. Wharton[27] describes the scientific and educational opportunities available in Georgia's Alcovy River swamp:

> The Alcovy River is ideally suited for educational uses: it is essentially unpolluted, it is located within easy driving distance of a large metropolitan area but is unaffected by it; and it contains a unique swamp ecosystem found nowhere else in the Georgia Piedmont.

Wharton goes on to describe the diversity of habitats present in the Alcovy riverine wetland and how it is suited for the study of not only biological processes but also geological and cultural concepts. Since the Alcovy river bottom is adapted to "annual catastrophism" from flooding, educational activities will likely not have any adverse impact on the ecosystem.

Considerable research on wetland ecosystems has been conducted by the Institute of Ecology at the University of Georgia and much is currently in progress. Research on salt marshes is being conducted at the Marine Institute on Sapelo Island. Freshwater wetlands are being studied at the Okefenokee Swamp. Research on the value of riverine vegetation in filtering agrichemicals and soils from farmland is included in a study being conducted at the USDA research center in Tifton. This long-term research is providing new and better insights into the structure and functions of wetland ecosystems.

As these research efforts identify the overall values associated with wetlands, the costs and benefits associated with the conversion of wetlands to other uses will become more readily identifiable.

The Worth of an Acre of Marsh

Because land use decisions are often made solely on the cash value of particular alternatives, a number of attempts have been made to place a dollar value on naturally functioning wetland environments. Due to the variability of wetlands and the assessment of both market and nonmarket values associated with wetlands, however, it is difficult to reach a consensus value. Also, the larger values of wetlands that relate to global life-support benefits usually accrue to society in general rather than to the individual landowner.

Much of the work in attempting to assign dollar values to wetlands has been conducted by Dr. Eugene Odum and his associates at the Institute of Ecology, University of Georgia[28] and his brother, Dr. Howard Odum, and his associates at the Center for Wetlands, University of Florida.[29] Early attempts to evaluate wetlands divided the values into four categories: (1) by-product production (fisheries, etc.); (2) potential for aquacultural development; (3) waste assimilation; and (4) total life-support value in terms of the "work of nature" as a function of primary production. The values of waste assimilation and total life-support work were estimates of what man would have to pay in terms of the value of useful work performed by an acre of marsh, should it not be available to do this work. These nonmarket values are several times higher than those which can be obtained from by-products, except possibly under intensive aquacultural development which in itself would eliminate recreational and most other uses.

More recent attempts to evaluate wetlands have focused more on energy. The common denominator used for comparing the value of wetlands to other ecosystems is, in Howard Odum's terms, "embodied energy," or the amount of energy necessary to produce the goods and services provided by the wetland. The values obtained by this method are in the same range as values obtained by simply totaling the noncompetitive values of the wetlands.

Through these efforts to identify the market and nonmarket values of wetlands, the Odums and their associates have found that, in general, the value of wetlands varies in accordance with the water fluctuation associated with the wetlands: the greater the water fluctuations, the greater the values. This applies both to salt marshes where water fluctuations are generally the result of tides and to freshwater wetlands where water fluctuations relate primarily to periodic inundations resulting from precipitation. In both cases, water movement represents an energy input to the system.

Although the types of products vary between salt marshes and freshwater wetlands, the former producing shrimp and other marine products and the latter producing terrestrial products such as wood and wildlife, the range of dollar values is similar. Most wetlands, simply by being wetlands, will provide a combination of market and nonmarket values that annually range from $10,000 to $30,000 per acre.

The similarity in values for both fresh and saltwater wetlands is of interest. Nationally and in Georgia, greater emphasis has been placed on protecting salt marshes than on protecting freshwater wetlands. This is likely the result of the more easily definable geographic location of salt marshes and the direct value associated with marine fisheries. But the fact that freshwater wetlands provide a similar range of values to society would indicate that they too should be provided at least comparable protection under the law.

Howard Odum states that this life-support value[30]

is a contribution to the public good that requires no individual human effort or right requiring payment. When land is bought and sold, perhaps the life-support rights should be retained by the public and not sold. Estimates of embodied energy and dollars suitable for evaluating the contribution of wetlands are not to be used in paying for land ownership, since the owner never did anything or paid anyone for the life-support part of the land's operation.

Whatever method used for evaluating wetlands that incorporates the non-market, life-support functions will show a significant value to society. The fact that this value is not reflected in the real estate value of the land encourages private owners to convert wetlands to nonwetland uses. If this forcing mechanism is to be changed, some way of separating these values will be required. Eugene Odum states:[31]

> What I am suggesting is that most inland wetlands, and many coastal ones of limited area as well, have their greatest value at the state or regional level, and hence should be dealt with politically and economically at this level. A small patch of wetland considered only as an isolated local ecosystem will in most cases have such a small value by whatever method of assessment one might adopt that preservation cannot possibly compete with other land use demands. When such a patch can be shown to be a vital functional part of a larger riverine, estuarine, lacustrine, ground water, or other regional system, then a much stronger case for preservation can be made.

Eugene Odum goes on to say that preservation of private wetlands would be accelerated if the tax system would recognize the nonmarket values as well as the market value. Such recognition would permit a tax deduction to owners who wish to donate property to public institutions for preservation purposes.

The question then of "What is an acre of marsh worth?" is a difficult one to answer. It depends on its size and relationship to other ecosystems, and on the embodied energy of that particular wetland, and on human demands being placed on it. It also depends on whether we consider only market values or the total market and nonmarket values of the wetland, and on how we attempt to assign these values. In any event, we know that the value of the wetland to society is much greater than it is to the individual landowner and that if the conversion of wetlands to nonwetland uses is to be discouraged, then mechanisms will have to be implemented that reflect the public interest.

The dichotomy of interests between the value to the private landowner and the value to society becomes an increasingly serious problem as population and industrial growth accelerate. If the wetland values determined by the Odums and their associates become generally recognized and accepted, then federal, state, and local governmental decision makers will be less likely to lease, give away, or sell valuable wetlands for development projects. Planners will also have greater incentive and public support for zoning such areas consistently with their value to the public interest.

WETLAND TRENDS

Until recently, there existed no reliable quantitative assessment of wetland resources in the United States and until very recently nothing was documented concerning what is now evidenced to be a precipitous decline in these resources. Increasing scientific recognition of the many types of wetland environments and the valuable functions they are capable of performing has underscored the need for accurate wetland resources data.

Since early European settlement of this country, wetlands have experienced continuous though fluctuating periods of acreage decline. An expanding population base imposing urban and agricultural development pressures combined with ignorance of the values associated with wetland environments have been major factors behind these losses. Recent information on wetland losses may help to reverse this trend.

Wetland Inventories

Over the years, a number of attempts have been made to quantify wetlands in the United States. These inventories were conducted by different federal agencies for different purposes.

1906 USDA Inventory

The first attempt to inventory wetlands in the United States was made in 1906 by the U.S. Department of Agriculture for the purpose of determining the agricultural potential of the nation's wetlands. For this reason, the inventory focused on those wetlands that could most easily be converted to agricultural purposes. This survey estimated that 79 million acres of swamps and overflowed land could be reclaimed for profitable agriculture.[32] In this inventory, no coastal wetlands were included, there was no classification of wetlands by types, and eight states were excluded from the survey.

1922 USDA Inventory

A second inventory was conducted in 1922 by the Bureau of Agricultural Economics of the U.S. Department of Agriculture. It was based on information related to highway construction, soil surveys, topographic maps produced by the U.S. Geological Survey, state reports, and the 1920 census of drainage. This inventory identified 91,543,000 acres of wetlands of which 7,363,000 were listed as tidal marsh and the remainder as inland wetlands.[33] The most complete inventory made until the most recent analysis conducted by the Fish and Wildlife Service, it included a breakdown of wetlands by vegetative type.

1940 Drainage Reconnaissance Survey

Based on a drainage reconnaissance survey, in 1940 the Soil Conservation Service estimated that there were 97,332,000 acres of ''wet, swampy and overflow land outside organized drainage enterprises.''[34]

1953 USDA Publication

In 1953, the USDA published a report which stated that there were some 125 million acres of undeveloped wet and swamp lands which were subject to overflow.[35]

1956 Fish and Wildlife Service Inventory

The first major survey of the nation's wetland resources, conducted by the U.S. Department of Interior's Fish and Wildlife Service (FWS) and published in 1956, is commonly known as "Circular 39."[36] The purpose of the survey was to determine

1. the location and extent of wetlands in each of the lower 48 states,
2. the wetland types in each area, and
3. their relative usefulness to wildlife, primarily waterfowl.

The 1956 FWS study inventoried only 74.4 million acres of the wetland habitat in the United States. Thus, not all wetlands were included. Although Georgia ranked third in total wetland acreage included, only a small percentage of these wetlands were rated of high or "primary" value to waterfowl (see Figure 2). A major contribution of this research effort was its categorization of wetlands into 20 basic types composing coastal fresh and saline areas and inland fresh and saline areas. This classification system has been replaced by the latest FWS analysis of wetlands and deepwater habitats, which includes 55 basic types (see page 6).

The 1956 FWS analysis, however, lacked several elements necessary to effectively analyze national wetland resources. For instance, the less favorable a wetland environment was for waterfowl habitat, the less likely it was to be included in the study, regardless of its value to local communities for flood protection or water quality maintenance. Furthermore, values assessed to wetland acreages were determined relative only to other wetland habitats *within that state*, and inconsistent considerations were employed for the breeding-range states of the Midwest and for the wintering habitat in the southern states. Thus, Circular 39 (by its own acknowledgement) did not put forth a common denominator for interstate comparisons of wetland values so as to further the development of a comprehensive national wetland management program. While Georgia and other state game and land use management efforts were able to be planned with respect to waterfowl protection, a resource base from which such planning could incorporate the many other wetland attributes of value to the public was absent.

1984 FWS National Wetlands Trends Survey

A more comprehensive investigation of the nation's wetland resources was accomplished by the Fish and Wildlife Service in 1984. This survey, conducted

Figure 2: *Wetlands of the Southeastern United States*

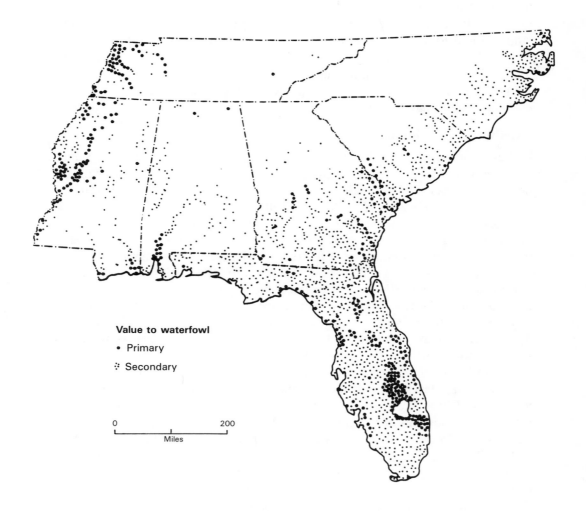

Value to waterfowl

• Primary

∴ Secondary

0   200

Miles

Adapted from FWS, *Wetlands of the United States,* 1956.

by the National Wetlands Inventory Project (NWI), consisted of random sampling and statistical analysis of wetlands and documented the wetland trends between the mid-1950s and the mid-1970s.[37] Information from this study is the most accurate and reliable available. The data have strong statistical validity for nationwide wetland losses and generally represent what happened to the resource prior to the implementation of the Clean Water Act's section 404 permit program, which regulates dredging and filling of wetlands. Although the results of this study are statistically reliable at the national level, at the state and substate level these data may be less reliable.

Distribution of Wetlands

As these inventories have shown, wetlands occur throughout the United States and comprise about 5 percent of the contiguous states. About 95 percent of the 90 million acres of wetlands in the lower 48 states are freshwater wetlands; the remainder being coastal, saltwater wetlands.[38]

Figure 3 presents the general distribution of wetlands in the United States. As this figure indicates, wetland distribution is dependent upon the geologic history and climatic conditions of the region. Generally, those areas that have greater topographic relief which allows water to run off will have fewer wetlands than those areas that are flat. Also, those areas that are geologically old are less likely to have wetlands since nature has had a longer time to fill in low spots or erode barriers that at one time dammed water and created wetlands. Humid areas like the southeastern United States are more likely to have wetlands than the more arid regions of the country.

Figure 4 shows the major physiographic regions in the United States. Since the eastern highlands, which include the Blue Ridge and Ridge and Valley provinces of Georgia, are geologically old and have generally steep slopes, fewer wetlands are found in this region. The FWS estimates that only 2 percent of the land area in the eastern highlands consists of wetlands. The Gulf-Atlantic Rolling Plain, which includes both the Piedmont and Upper Coastal Plain provinces in Georgia, has less topographic relief and more wetlands. About 8 percent of the land area in this region consists of wetlands. The Atlantic Coastal Flats or Lower Coastal Plain which, as the name implies, has very little relief, contains the highest percentage of wetlands. Some 36 percent of the land area in this region is classified as wetlands. The wetlands along the coast include both fresh and salt water types. About 16 percent of this land area is designated as wetlands.[39]

Quantitative Losses

The Fish and Wildlife Service estimates the conterminous United States to have originally contained 215 million acres of fresh and salt water wetlands.[40] By the mid-1950s this acreage was reduced to an estimated 108.1 million acres.

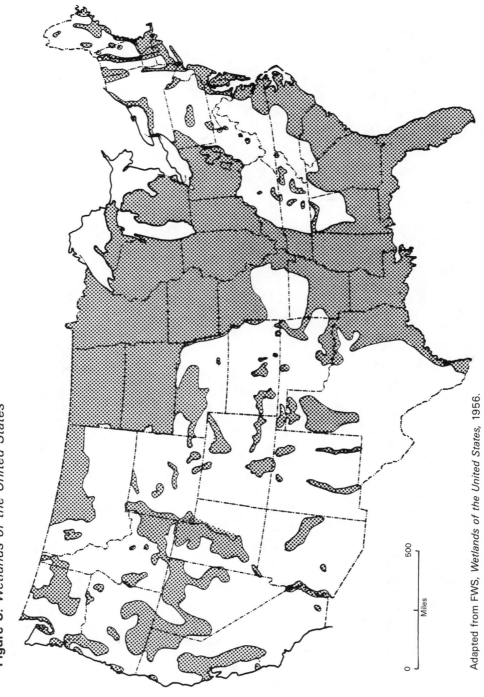

Figure 3: *Wetlands of the United States*

Adapted from FWS, *Wetlands of the United States,* 1956.

500

Miles

0

Figure 4: *Major Physiographic Regions of the United States*

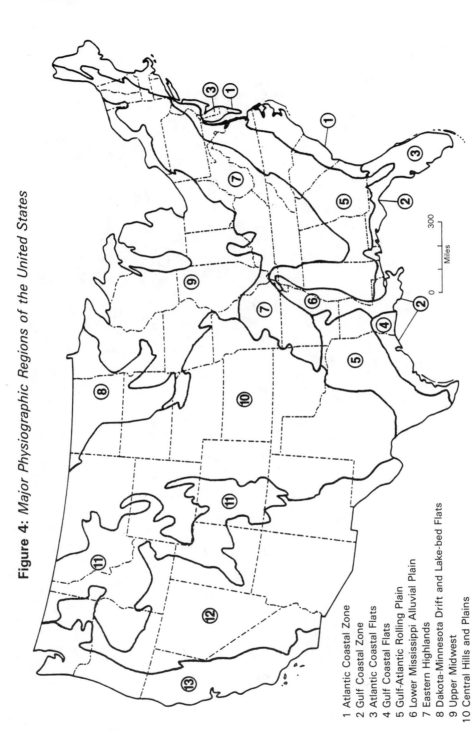

1 Atlantic Coastal Zone
2 Gulf Coastal Zone
3 Atlantic Coastal Flats
4 Gulf Coastal Flats
5 Gulf-Atlantic Rolling Plain
6 Lower Mississippi Alluvial Plain
7 Eastern Highlands
8 Dakota-Minnesota Drift and Lake-bed Flats
9 Upper Midwest
10 Central Hills and Plains
11 Rocky Mountains
12 Intermontane
13 Pacific Mountains

Office of Technology Assessment, *Wetlands: Their Use and Regulation*, 1984.

Despite minor gains from reservoir construction, beaver activity, and irrigation and marsh creation projects, the next 20 years evidenced a decline to 99 million acres of remaining wetlands.[41] Consequently, over 54 percent of the original resource has been converted to other uses. The average rate of wetland conversion from the mid-1950s to the mid-1970s is 458,000 acres per year, an area roughly equal to half the size of Rhode Island.

Freshwater wetlands bore the brunt of these impacts, averaging a loss rate of 440,000 acres per year, while saltwater wetlands lost about 18,000 acres per year during the same 20-year period. Of the remaining 99 million acres nationally, the FWS found palustrine or freshwater wetlands to comprise 95 percent of the wetlands. Over one-half of the nation's freshwater wetlands are forested and almost one-third are emergent wetlands. Slightly more than 5 percent of all wetland areas are estuarine or salt water.[42]

Causes of Wetland Loss

Quantitative losses and the qualitative degradation of wetland environments is attributable to many human activities and several natural occurrences. Table 2 lists the major factors causing wetland conversion to other uses. Qualitative alterations such as lowering of water levels and water pollution serve to degrade wetland resources by reducing the effectiveness with which they perform the beneficial functions previously outlined. Wetland degradation may be site-specific, requiring a very local level of management and control, or it may be widespread as with the Chesapeake Bay, requiring multistate efforts to improve the situation.

Quantitative impacts on wetlands from various agents of conversion are more easily identified and are, consequently, capable of reasonably accurate assessment through the use of techniques such as remote sensing. Many wetland studies have identified the sources of conversion, but the National Wetland Inventory and a subsequent analysis conducted by the Office of Technology Assessment[43] provide the most recent analyses of the sources of major impact.

According to the FWS,[44] the vast majority of wetland losses from the mid-1950s to the mid-1970s were the direct result of drainage for crop and timber production. As would be expected, agricultural conversion of wetlands has had a greater impact on freshwater wetlands, with 80 percent of freshwater conversions going to agriculture. Conversely, agriculture contributed to only 2 percent of all saltwater wetland losses. Although urban development produced relatively minor impacts on freshwater wetlands, the overwhelming nationwide trends of growth in coastal areas is reflected in the rather large proportion of saltwater wetlands converted to urban land use (22 percent) and port development (56 percent).

Natural influences affecting wetlands include rising sea levels, the local hydrological cycle, natural succession and fire, and beaver dam construction.

Table 2: *Causes of Wetland Loss and Degradation*

Human Threats

Direct:

Drainage for crop production, timber production, and mosquito control.

Dredging and stream channelization for navigation channels, flood protection, coastal housing development, and reservoir maintenance.

Filling for dredged spoil and other solid waste disposal; roads and highways; and commercial, residential, and industrial development.

Construction of dikes, dams, levees, and seawalls for flood control, water supply, irrigation, and storm protection.

Discharges of materials (e.g., pesticides, herbicides, other pollutants, nutrient loading from domestic sewage and agricultural runoff, and sediments from dredging and filling, agricultural and other land development) into waters and wetlands.

Mining of wetland soils for peat, coal, sand, gravel, phosphate, and other materials.

Indirect:

Sediment diversion by dams, deep channels, and other structures.

Hydrologic alterations by canals, spoil banks, roads, and other structures.

Subsidence due to extraction of ground water, oil, gas, sulphur, and other minerals.

Natural Threats

Subsidence (including natural rise of sea level).

Droughts.

Hurricanes and other storms.

Erosion.

Biotic effects (e.g., muskrat, nutria, and goose "eat-outs").

From U.S. Fish and Wildlife Service, Wetlands of the United States: Current Status and Recent Trends, 1984.

Although rising sea levels may permanently inundate wetlands at the lowest elevations, previously drier upland areas may take on their former role. Likewise, hurricanes can substantially alter coastal geographic and vegetative patterns. Natural succession, fire, and periodic hydrological fluctuations typically alter wetlands without the imposition of any net loss or gain. Beavers create wetlands by damming stream channels.

Unlike natural wetland perturbations, human activities are largely destructive to these environments. Wetlands may be important to such activities as agriculture, forestry, port and harbor development, oil and gas extraction, urban growth, mineral and other mining operations, and water resource development. Activities involving drainage, filling, dredging, and flooding produce the most permanent wetland impacts. Water diversions and pollution can have similar effects although degradation is usually the immediate result.

Dredging and Excavation

Dredging and excavation each involve the direct removal of wetland soil and vegetation. They are responsible for the significant wetland losses associated with agricultural conversion, along with mosquito control ditching; canal construction; peat, gravel and phosphate mining; and port development and maintenance. In coastal areas, dredging can affect not only the immediate wetland area but can increase tidal ranges in the upper reaches of estuaries, and initiate persistent canal bank erosion. Excavation is generally a technique used for mining and to create "dugouts" or irrigation reservoir pits. Total removal of vegetation is common to peat, phosphate, and limestone mining[45] and, where ground water refills the pit, can result in lowering of the ground water table or blockage of surface water flows.[46] The excavation of "dugouts," or irrigation reuse pits, results in the partial drainage of some wetlands and the flooding of others.[47] In Nebraska, such wetland losses have led to an increased incidence or risk of disease to waterfowl and a reduction in food supply and breeding habitat for migratory birds.[48]

Filling

Often closely associated with dredging activities is the filling of wetlands. This is the case in coastal states where waterfront real estate may be created by the excavation of canals within wetlands, using the dredged material as fill for building sites. Area elevation is increased, wetland vegetation is destroyed, and canals are less productive for fish and shellfish communities. Wetlands are also one of the repositories of fill generated by the Corps of Engineers' maintenance of the intercoastal waterway and tidal river areas.[49]

Other materials used for fill include municipal waste, construction and demolition debris, broken concrete from highway construction, and coal ash.[50] Some types of fill material may present serious risks of chemical contamination to the wetlands and associated streams or ground water.

Draining and Clearing

Drainage of wetlands and subsequent clearing is a major factor in wetland conversions, especially in the southeastern United States. Small drainage ditches are effective at channeling surface water runoff and lowering ground water levels such that agricultural and forestry operations may more easily harvest their respective products or crops. After harvesting, the area may be allowed to regenerate or be artificially reforested to commercially desirable species. Professional forest management practices can increase the yield of marketable timber such as pine from the former wetland, although sustained biological productivity is reduced because of reduced nutrient inflows. An increasing demand for pine products in Georgia is creating a considerable incentive to clear and drain the state's bottomland hardwood wetlands.

Wetland drainage and clearing activities can degrade public water and wildlife resources and affect the landowners downstream. Drainage ditches for agricultural crops, as would be expected, have been found to increase the runoff of pesticides, herbicides, fertilizers, and animal wastes.[51] Soil fertility is also reduced by the loss of organic material due to oxidation.[52] If good management practices are not used, soil erosion and sedimentation may also result. Surface water contaminations may develop into water quality problems for downstream municipalities, industries, and agricultural users. In addition, drainage of wetlands associated with streams and rivers (riverine wetlands) may increase the danger of flooding of public and private properties in downstream areas.

Bottomland hardwood forests and other wetlands are prime habitats for many species of birds and mammals that hunters and others rely on for recreation. Also, these riverine wetlands can serve as critical spawning grounds for many commercially important species of fish that the coastal fishery industries rely on for their livelihood. Drainage and clearing activities impose major reductions on the diversity of wildlife.[53] In times of severe drought, loss of such habitat can be devastating to wildlife species dependent on isolated freshwater resources provided by wetlands.

Flooding and Water Withdrawals

Depending on depth, permanent flooding of wetlands will eliminate wetland vegetation. Flooding is usually accomplished by impoundments restricting downstream water flow. The purposes of such impoundments include water supply reservoirs for municipal and agricultural users, hydroelectric power generation, flood control for downstream properties, waterfowl management, mosquito control, and aquaculture. In addition, downstream wetlands may suffer washouts due to sustained releases from large upstream reservoirs.

Water flow restrictions by reservoirs can dewater downstream wetlands. In coastal areas, decreasing freshwater flow into estuaries allows encroachment of saline water inland and reduces the influx of detritus and nutrients into the estuarine food chain. Harvestable fishery resources are thereby endangered by loss of breeding habitat and loss of food availability. In freshwater areas, upstream depletions can lower the water levels of downstream wetlands, thus devaluating wildlife habitat.

Dewatering of wetlands is the intentional result of dikes and flood control levees that retain floodflows within the river channel. As a result, velocity of storm runoff is increased, scouring and erosion is increased, flood storage capacity is lost, and the chance of downstream flooding is increased.[54]

Pollution of Wetlands

Wetlands can be polluted in terms of quantity and quality of foreign input. Excessive quantities of water can suffocate wetland vegetation. If the water level is raised sufficiently, an open body of water can result from the decay and eventual collapse of forested wetland vegetation or from mere coverage of emergent wetlands.

Upstream erosion from mismanaged forestry, agriculture, or development practices can increase the quantity of suspended sediments deposited on the wetland floor. Sediment buildup can then reduce flood storage capacities, increase levels of sediment-bound toxins, and eventually fill in the wetland depression. Urban stormwater and contaminated dredge spoil can also pollute wetland systems. Urban runoff has been specifically shown to detrimentally affect tidal wetlands around Hilton Head, South Carolina.[55]

Pollutants in general, and contaminated dredge spoil in particular, are dangerous in that they can be periodically resuspended.[56] Although bioavailability of many toxic contaminants may be quite low, many do not degrade and thus may present long-term threats for bioaccumulation within the food chain.[57]

Wetlands have been used to purify municipal and other wastewater of nutrients and suspended solids. Adverse effects can result from excessive nutrients such that species composition is altered and wetland eutrophication is initiated. Research indicates that about 250 acres of wetlands are required to assimilate one million gallons of sewage per day.[58]

SUMMARY

Our understanding of wetlands is increasing. We now are better able to classify wetlands. We can better define and delimit these wetlands based on hydrologic, vegetative, and soil characteristics. We are able to identify and assign to wetlands a wide variety of environmental quality, fish and wildlife, and socioeconomic values. We also know that there has been a significant decline in wetlands nationally, amounting to a loss of 55 percent of the original wetlands in this country. Major causes of the conversion of wetlands to other uses include agricultural and forestry practices, urban development, dredging and filling for navigation purposes, and flood control projects. The overall costs and benefits of these conversions have not been determined.

3 Georgia Wetlands

Since the earliest days of settlement in Georgia, wetlands have played an important role, both positive and negative, in the state. Wetlands were the setting for early rice plantations along the coast and for plume hunting to supply "Gay Nineties" millineries. They were also a source of pestilence and an impediment to travel and development. The recent increase in understanding of wetland values and the documentation of a significant national decline in wetland acreage have aroused concern over the status of Georgia wetlands. The following discussion of the types and distribution of wetlands in Georgia presents a conceptual framework for their study, identifying specific wetlands of value and analyzing wetland trends in the state.

In the mid-1950s, the U.S. Fish and Wildlife Service (FWS) ranked Georgia third nationally behind Florida and Louisiana in total assessed acres of wetlands.[1] About 8 percent of the total national wetlands included in the analysis were located in Georgia. As indicated in Table 3, most of these were considered of marginal value for waterfowl purposes. The wetlands classified as having the greatest waterfowl value were the riverine wetlands along the Altamaha and other Coastal Plain rivers (see Figure 2, page 19). This analysis was fairly subjective, however, and did not include values of wetlands other than those for waterfowl habitat. In the mid-1970s, Georgia still ranked among the leading states in total wetland acreage, behind Florida, Louisiana, and North Carolina (see Figure 5).

Table 3: *Value of Wetlands to Waterfowl*

Acreage with value assessed as:	High	Moderate	Low	Negligible	Total
Georgia	20,900	440,400	1,428,900	4,029,300	5,919,500
United States	8,819,900	13,616,500	24,087,700	27,915,200	74,439,300

From U.S. Fish and Wildlife Service, *Wetlands of the United States,* Circular 39, 1956.

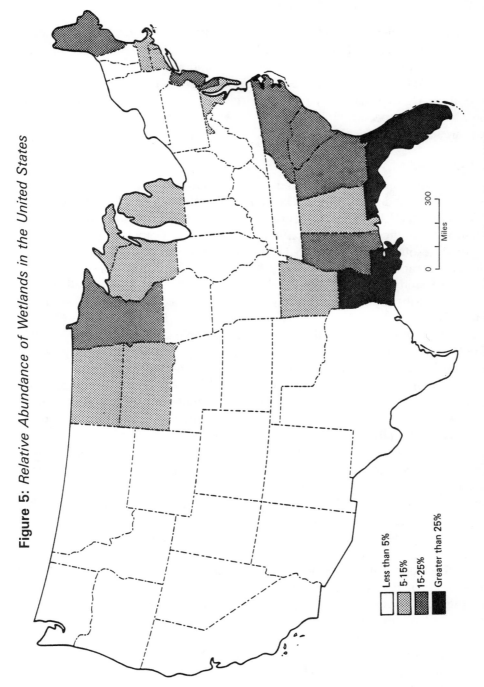

Figure 5: *Relative Abundance of Wetlands in the United States*

Less than 5%

5-15%

15-25%

Greater than 25%

300

Miles

0

FWS, *Wetlands of the United States: Current Status and Recent Trends,* 1984.

CURRENT ACREAGE OF WETLANDS IN GEORGIA

Although a detailed statewide inventory of wetlands in Georgia has not been conducted, besides the FWS National Wetlands Inventory, two recent land use analyses including wetland acreage have been undertaken. The methodologies of the two studies vary and as a result are not directly comparable to each other or to the FWS analysis. They provide insight into the wetland situation in the state, however, especially in that unlike the FWS assessment these studies provide breakdowns of wetland distributions within the state.

Methodology

The two studies quantifying wetland acreage in Georgia were conducted during the late 1970s and early 1980s. One was undertaken by the U.S. Department of Agriculture (USDA) Soil Conservation Service (SCS) pursuant to authorization by the Resources Conservation Act of 1977.[2] This act provided for an ongoing National Resources Inventory (NRI) to maintain a common data base for planning conservation programs. The 1982 NRI (reported in 1984) is the most exhaustive study of land use conditions ever undertaken by the USDA.

Soil Conservation Service personnel collected data on nonfederal land, using randomly selected 160-acre "primary sample units." Field investigations were conducted at three sample points within each sample unit, amounting to nearly 25,000 individually sampled points within Georgia alone. Reliability of this sampling system allows results to be accurately reported for each major land resource area (MLRA) of Georgia. Georgia's MLRAs, shown in Figure 6, are characterized by particular patterns of soil, climate, and water resources.

At each sampling point, SCS personnel recorded soil conditions according to the land capability classification system. Land capability is an interpretation that expresses the suitability of a soil for normal agricultural production. Capability classes are designated by Roman numerals I–VIII, the higher numerals indicating progressively greater limitations, and they are further divided into capability subclasses, indicating the type of limitation primarily responsible for its reduced agricultural potential. Thus, a soil of capability subclass "IIw" would have minor agricultural limitations due to wetness of the soil; capability subclass "VIIw" would have very severe limitations because of soil wetness.

SCS personnel also classified the same sample point as one of the 20 wetland types designated in the 1956 FWS Circular 39 wetland classification system (see Figure 1, page. 6). The data recorded in the field were then computerized by the staff of Iowa State University's Statistical Laboratory.

With the assistance of SCS personnel in the Georgia office in Athens, the NRI computer base was tapped in an attempt to quantify wetland resources in Georgia. The input methodology described above allowed the data to be extracted on the statewide and MLRA level for each of the wetland types found

Figure 6: *Major Land Resource Areas in Georgia*

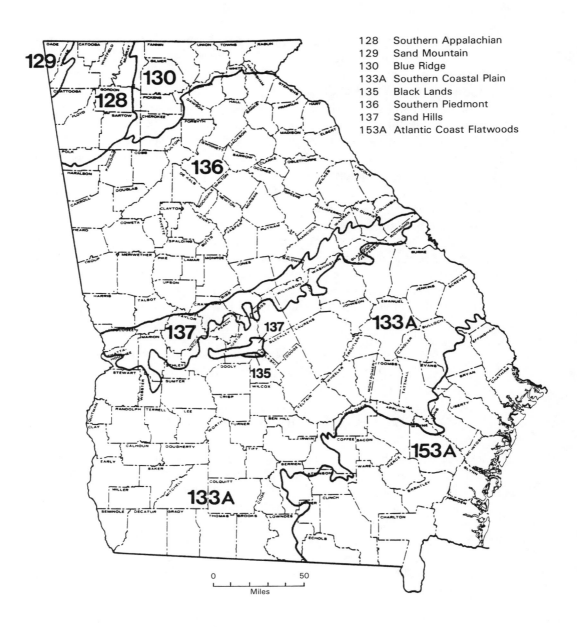

128   Southern Appalachian
129   Sand Mountain
130   Blue Ridge
133A Southern Coastal Plain
135   Black Lands
136   Southern Piedmont
137   Sand Hills
153A Atlantic Coast Flatwoods

USDA Soil Conservation Service.

in the state. Each wetland type was aligned with the various soil capability classes in which it was found. Thus, for each wetland type, acreage totals were found for different capability subclasses, subclasses whose major limitation was usually wet soil.

Based on advice and consultation with SCS personnel, Georgia wetland acreages were recorded for each wetland type represented by capability subclasses whose major limitation was wet or flooded soils. Totals were derived for the state as a whole and for each MLRA.

The second study of land use, consisting of an analysis of the Landsat digital data, was undertaken by the Georgia Department of Natural Resources in cooperation with the Georgia Institute of Technology. The methodology consisted of analyzing the composition of reflected radiation (brightness) from satellite tapes, using helicopters to verify information and compiling data based on 1.1 acre cells.[3] This approach is, therefore, an analysis of land cover type rather than land use (i.e., light reflected from a forest and a tree-covered park might be indistinguishable).

Results of this analysis were compiled for each county and released in an unpublished report entitled, "Georgia Statewide Landsat Classification Statistics by Counties."[4] Since only one statewide Landsat analysis has been undertaken, wetland trends are not discernible from this data set.

The methodologies used in the two studies vary considerably and consequently, direct comparisons are not possible. While Landsat data are based on acre by acre cover type, the SCS data are the result of sample site investigations extrapolated to estimate wetland acreage for each MLRA. Additionally, the nature of the Landsat data set allows wetland acreage figures to be reported for each county. The land areas used for presentation of data, counties and MLRAs, do not directly coincide, so for the purposes of presentation we have attempted to compile both data sets by MLRA, to enable discussion of the results.

The FWS National Wetland Inventory used a third methodology. This included an analysis of four square-mile sample units in each stratum or region, which are not directly comparable to MLRA or physiographic province. These are assigned proportionally by the expected wetland density as determined by earlier work. Georgia included 206 sample units. Analysis entailed comparisons of mid-1950s and mid-1970s aerial photographs of each sample unit, classification of wetlands by type, and determination of wetland trends.[5] Results of the National Wetland Inventory are utilized in this report to convey statewide wetland information, and Landsat and SCS data are employed to estimate wetland acreage within the state.

Distribution and Types of Wetlands in Georgia

Table 4 presents the total wetland acreage in Georgia as estimated by the FWS's National Wetlands Inventory, the DNR Landsat analysis, and the SCS National

Table 4: *Total Wetland Acreage in Georgia According to Three Estimates*

Analysis	Acres
Georgia Department of Natural Resources with Georgia Institute of Technology analysis of Landsat digital data	3,513,789
USDA Soil Conservation Service (SCS)	4,831,300
U.S. Fish and Wildlife Service (FWS)	5,298,000

Resources Inventory. Differences in acreage totals reflect differences in methodologies and assumptions used in statistical analysis. A possible explanation for the comparatively low Landsat total acreage is the difficulty in distinguishing forested wetland cover from that of other forest types, and nonforested wetland from pastures and cultivated lands, especially during dry periods. With the inclusion of federal lands and open water acreage in the SCS analysis, totals from this study would approach those of the FWS analysis. All these analyses provide insights into the wetland situation in the state but none is sufficiently accurate to determine the exact amount of wetland acreage in Georgia. At this time, the best estimates indicate that there are about 5 million acres of wetlands in Georgia—about 13 percent of the state.

The Landsat data and SCS data describe the distribution of wetlands within the state. For purposes of comparison, it is necessary to combine the categories so that all noncoastal freshwater wetlands are reported here as "forested wetlands." Coastal wetlands include both saltwater marshes and the freshwater marshes that feed them. Since the SCS data were organized according to soil types, no quantification of open water bodies was included in this study. Landsat data, however, should give an accurate picture of open water acreage in Georgia. Table 5 presents a comparison of wetlands in Georgia by MLRA as identified by the Landsat and SCS studies.

Although variation exists between the two data sets, comparable trends are apparent. The data show that Georgia is dimorphic with respect to wetlands. The northern portion of the state, including the Ridge and Valley, Blue Ridge, and Piedmont provinces, has few wetlands while the Coastal Plain has extensive wetlands. This is supported by the FWS analysis of wetlands by major regions in the country. The disparity in wetland location and concentration is important from a management standpoint in that half the state has so few wetlands that people may not appreciate their value while the other half of the state has so many wetlands that they may be seen as a nuisance.

Counties with the highest concentration of wetlands are: Chatham, McIntosh, Camden, Ware, Glynn, and Liberty. These counties are primarily coastal and the wetlands include the coastal marshes. Counties with high concentrations of freshwater wetlands are: Ware, Charlton, Burke, Clinch, Wayne,

Table 5: *Wetlands in Georgia by MLRA*

MLRA	Open Water	Forested Wetlands	Coastal Marsh	Total Wetlands
Ridge & Valley				
Landsat	8,445	0	0	8,445
SCS	— *	0	0	0
Blue Ridge				
Landsat	12,358	0	0	12,358
SCS	—	1,900	0	1,900
Piedmont				
Landsat	167,494	143,480	0	310,974
SCS	—	27,400	0	27,400
Sand Hills				
Landsat	13,574	72,376	0	85,950
SCS	—	54,600	0	54,600
Upper Coastal Plain				
Landsat	75,307	1,378,793	0	1,454,100
SCS	—	889,900	0	889,900
Lower Coastal Plain				
Landsat	205,861	809,206	626,921	1,641,988
SCS	—	1,487,800	380,000**	1,867,200
Total				
Landsat	483,039	2,403,855	626,921	3,513,815
SCS	—	2,461,600***	380,000	2,841,600

*U.S. Soil and Conservation Service data include *no* figures for open water.
**SCS "Coastal Marsh" includes Circular 39 types 12, 13; otherwise salt coastal marshes total 366,000 acres.
***SCS "Forested Wetlands" excludes types 2-4 (totaling nearly 2 million acres of emergent wetlands).

Thomas, Screven, Brooks, Long, and Lowndes. The Appendix lists wetland acreage by county as identified by the Landsat analysis.

Conceptualized Wetland Systems

For the purpose of conceptualizing the types of wetlands in Georgia, they are divided into four major categories: coastal wetlands including salt, brackish, and freshwater wetlands; the Okefenokee system; riverine wetlands; and inland wetlands. This is an oversimplification of the real world resource for purposes of presentation. For a more detailed description of wetlands in Georgia see Wharton,[6] who identified 39 hydrologic systems in the state.

Coastal Wetlands

The coastal region serves as a broad transition zone between the marine environment and the terrestrial environment. An integral part of this transition is the wetland environments that comprise a continuum from salt to fresh water. In the coastal region, identification of salt and brackish water marshes is facilitated by the vegetation, dominated by a limited number of species of marsh plants (*Spartina* and *Juncus,* respectively). Freshwater wetlands that interact with these salt marshes are more varied and somewhat difficult to identify. Figure 7 presents the coastal wetlands in Georgia.

This coastal marshland system was estimated by Johnson and his associates to include 393,000 acres, of which 286,000 acres were covered by *Spartina*.[7] These figures did not include the freshwater wetlands that feed the salt and brackish marshes. According to the Landsat data which includes open water estuaries, this system comprises 626,921 acres along the Georgia coast. Table 6 presents the breakdown in wetland acreage by type within the coastal zone of Georgia.

Table 6: *Coastal Wetlands in Georgia*

Wetland Type		Acres
Spartina		312,736
Juncus		185,346
Nonforested		128,839
	Total	626,921

From Georgia Department of Natural Resources, 1979.

The values of the coastal marshes have been well documented by Johnson *et al.*,[8] Wharton,[9] Odum,[10] and others. The salt and brackish coastal marshes have been afforded considerable protection by the Marshlands Protection Act of 1970, which requires a permit from the Georgia Department of Natural Resources to alter the marshes. This provides assurance that activities adversely affecting coastal marshes will be limited.

The freshwater wetland system which interacts with the salt marshes is not considered under the Marshlands Protection Act. This system is important in providing an influx of nutrients, and of fresh water to dilute saline water from the sea. Many aquatic organisms such as oysters depend on a relatively narrow range of salt concentration and without sufficient freshwater input the system would be altered considerably.

Actual and potential threats to the coastal marsh system include urban and second-home development pressure; industrial activities; mining of phosphates; dredging, filling, diking and ditching of marshes for navigation and other purposes; and alterations of the coastal riverine systems which interact with these marsh systems.[11]

Figure 7: *Coastal Wetlands in Georgia*

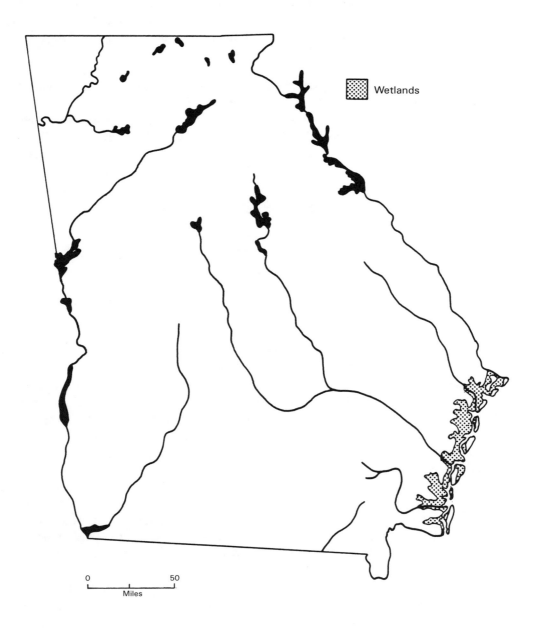

The Okefenokee System

The Okefenokee Swamp encompasses 467,157 acres in southeastern Georgia and extends slightly into Florida (see Figure 8).[12] Besides being a large wetland system, it is separated from other wetlands in the state, receiving about 83 percent of its water from rainfall and only about 15 percent from surface water.[13] Outflow from the Okefenokee is through the Suwannee River and St. Marys River.

The Okefenokee (an Indian name translated as ''land of the trembling earth'') is a basin situated on a relatively impervious substrate of Pliocene and Miocene clay covered by medium- to fine-grained sand and peat deposits. The Okefenokee is believed to have been formed when a marine bay was isolated from the ocean by the development of a longshore barrier island, the present Trail Ridge.[14] As sea levels dropped, the ridge dammed the basin forming the swamp.[15] The swamp contains open water, prairies, shrubland, and forest. If undisturbed, it would eventually become either a mixed black gum or bay swamp.[16]

Natural fires caused by lightning occur regularly in dry periods. According to Wharton,[17] the Okefenokee receives more lightning than any other region of Georgia. After the 1954 drought, however, during which fires burned 284,000 acres of the swamp, a 4.5 mile water control structure (sill) was constructed on the Suwannee River to maintain water levels in the swamp.

Attempts have been made to drain the Okefenokee for agriculture, and much of the swamp has been logged over. The Georgia and Suwannee Land and Canal Company dug a canal 45 feet wide and 6 feet deep in 1891 to drain the swamp for agricultural purposes but, after completing 12 miles of it, abandoned the project when water flowed the wrong way.[18] Logging by the Hebard Lumber Company ceased operations in 1927 after removing over .5 billion cubic yards of timber, primarily cypress.[19]

In 1937, President Franklin D. Roosevelt established the Okefenokee as a refuge, later named the Okefenokee National Wildlife Refuge. The refuge contains 396,315 acres, or about 85 percent of the swamp. The state of Georgia owns a portion of the swamp, the Stephen C. Foster State Park. In 1974, additional protection was given when 353,981 acres (nearly 90 percent of the refuge) were included in the National Wilderness Preservation System.[20] As a result of this public ownership, the Okefenokee is now protected from conversion pressures.

Riverine Wetlands

Riverine wetlands are often referred to as floodplains or bottomlands. They comprise the land area adjacent to streams and rivers that are periodically flooded. Approximately one quarter of the hydrologic systems identified by Wharton[21] in Georgia are riverine type systems. These systems are characterized

Figure 8: *Okefenokee Swamp*

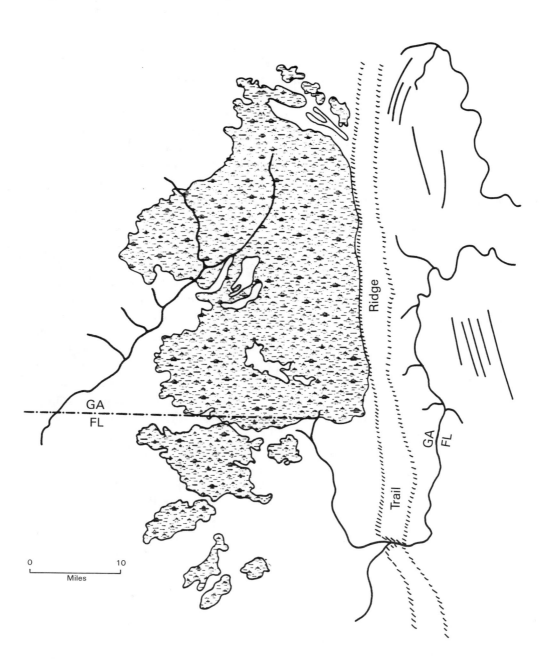

by the import and export of soil and organic matter which, depending on the system, may make them very productive biologically.

Major rivers in Georgia tend to flow in a north-south direction and, as a result, traverse the major physiographic regions of the state. As they flow through these provinces, the rivers change from rapidly flowing, white water streams in the mountains to larger, sediment-laden rivers in the Piedmont to slow, meandering rivers in the Coastal Plain. As the rivers go through this metamorphosis, so do their floodplains. Floodplains in the northern part of the state tend to be narrow, steep-sided valleys, usually less than one-half mile, while in the Coastal Plain they tend to be broad, flat bottoms, reaching several miles in width (see Figure 9).

This flow of rivers from north Georgia to the Coastal Plain provides nutrients and organic matter to the floodplains. One of the major characteristics of these river swamps is their fluctuating water levels, producing annual pulses of nutrient fertility and biological activity. This fertility is a result of organic material decomposed by alternate wetting and drying, biological action, and the influx of mineral nutrients brought in as silts or clays. For most Georgia rivers and streams the period of high water levels is in the winter and spring.[22]

Rivers originating in the Coastal Plain province do not receive this influx of nutrients from the Piedmont and are generally much less productive. These are referred to as ''black water'' streams because the tannins make the deep water appear black, while shallower water will appear reddish in color.

Riverine wetlands are important for a number of reasons (see Chapter 2). Because of the input of nutrient materials, mineral levels in these wetlands may be more than 10 times greater than in the adjacent flatwoods. Consequently, biological productivity is high.[23] Hydrologically, flood waters are held and pollutants and silt are filtered out by these riverine systems. As a result, they have a beneficial effect on both water quantity and water quality.

Threats to riverine wetlands vary with location. In the northern half of the state, major threats are urban and residential development and dam construction. Severe development pressure is being exerted along the Chattahoochee River in Atlanta and along various streams in the north Georgia mountains. Since the bulk of the state's population growth is projected to occur in the Piedmont region, the demand to build in the floodplains will increase. In the north Georgia area, which is experiencing second home development and tourist related growth pressures, cities such as Helen and Clayton already show considerable development occurring in floodplains.

As water needs mount with increasing population and industrial development, there will be added demand for reservoir construction to provide additional water, and possibly for hydroelectric generation sites. Construction of reservoirs will inundate riverine systems. These dams may aid in flood protection, but the other values associated with these wetlands will be lost.

Figure 9: *Riverine Wetlands in Georgia*

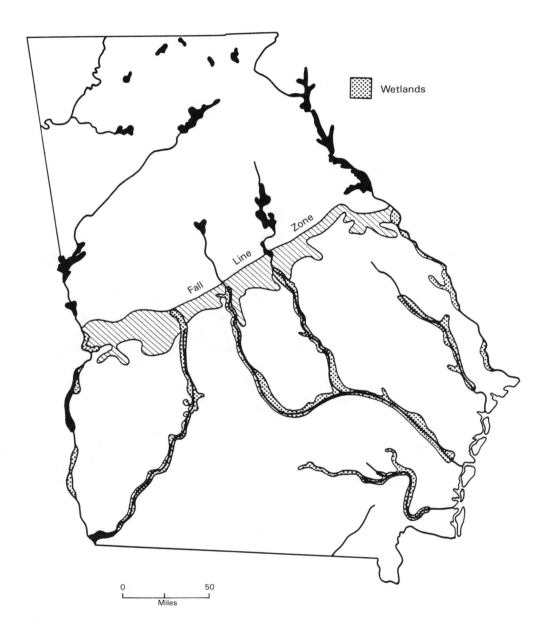

In the Coastal Plain, drainage of riverine systems for pine and agricultural production appears to be the major conversion activity. Since the productivity of these riverine wetlands depends on the fluctuating water levels depositing nutrients on the soil, to drain them for forestry and agricultural production would alter the water regime and result in a reduction in productivity. Channelization of Coastal Plain rivers for navigation can have a severe effect on both the hydrology and biological productivity of the riverine systems.

Inland Wetlands

Inland wetlands include cypress and gum ponds, Carolina bays, limesinks, and other naturally occurring freshwater wetlands not directly associated with riverine systems or the coastal marshes. Because of their variety and distribution throughout the Coastal Plain, these inland wetlands are valuable for maintaining plant and animal diversity within the region and for their interrelationship with both surface and ground water systems.

Cypress and gum ponds. Occurring throughout the Coastal Plain province, cypress and gum ponds extend occasionally into the Piedmont province. Generally they occupy impermeable basins underlain by clay or hardpan. The distinguishing feature of these wetlands is the type of vegetation which dominates them: cypress or black gum. Water fluctuations may be less in gum ponds than in cypress ponds. It is estimated that there are hundreds of thousands of cypress and gum ponds in southern Georgia, the cypress being more common.[24]

Wharton[25] concluded that "even the smallest cypress and gum ponds are veritable storehouses of animal life and focal points for the animal communities of the surrounding pinelands. . . .The ponds maintain not only their own food webs, but the life web of the pinelands of the southern Coastal Plain and sandhill areas." These ponds vary considerably in size, water regime, rate and amount of peat deposition, and plant and animal life.

Cypress and gum ponds are important hydrologically in serving to recharge the surficial aquifer in the eastern part of the Coastal Plain and the major aquifers (Floridan, Cretaceous and Clayton) where they occur near the surface. Although these ponds are often considered isolated from riverine wetlands, they may have a role in recharging surface water flow.

The major threat to cypress and gum ponds by far is drainage for pine production.[26] Wharton[27] contends, however, that these drained ponds grow pines very slowly. Howard Odum and his associates[28] concluded that in view of their hydrological values, their value in controlling fire, their potential for waste assimilation, their ability to produce quality hardwood timber, and their indispensable wildlife support functions, cypress and gum ponds should not be drained.

Carolina bays. Carolina bays are elliptical or oval wetlands of various sizes which, along with cypress and gum ponds, compose the major inland wetland resources in the Coastal Plain (see Figure 10). More than 1,000 bays occupying about 250,000 acres have been mapped by the Georgia Geologic Survey.[29] Besides being elliptical in shape, Carolina bays are generally found in sandy terrain, have a blue clay layer, are all aligned in a northeast-southwest manner, with raised sandy rims on the south and east edges. Because of these similarities, it is speculated that all Carolina bays were formed at the same time and under similar conditions. Possible causes of their formation include a meteor shower or gale force winds scooping out sand during the last glaciation.[30]

Because of the variation in size and water depths of Carolina bays, they support a variety of biotic communities. Since the water levels are generally shallow, however, many have been drained for crop production and most have been logged of their original timber. Because of their scientific interest and biological diversity, Wharton[31] suggested that a wide spectrum of bay types should be preserved.

Limesinks or sinkholes. Limesinks or sinkholes occur in areas where soluble bedrock such as limestone and dolomite lies near the land surface (see Figure 10). In Georgia this includes the Dougherty Plain region, the Valdosta area, and along the Fall Line, the kaolin region. Limesinks can also be found in the northwest part of the state in the Ridge and Valley province.[32]

When water comes in contact with rocks such as limestone and dolomite, the rock material will be dissolved by the water. Over the eons, this will result in the formation of seepage channels and caverns. When ground water levels decline due to increased withdrawals or decreased recharge during drought periods the roof of the cavern may collapse forming a depression. As water levels return to normal, the limesink will form a pond or wetland.

Limesinks are important hydrologically. Because of the mechanics of their formation, unless they are plugged by an impervious material, they serve as a direct conduit between the surface and the ground water. Contaminants can easily be carried through the sinkhole to pollute the ground water. As a result, limesinks are a major concern from a water quality standpoint.

Because of their variability, limesinks support a diverse array of plant and animal life. In fact, some of the cypress and gum ponds previously discussed are limesinks and the biotic values associated with these ponds also apply to limesinks.[33]

Major threats to these important wetlands are associated with agricultural production since they are concentrated in the major agricultural region of the state. Drainage and filling activities to enable the wetland to be used for agricultural production destroy the wetland. The use of agrichemicals in this area coupled with the ground water recharge potential of limesinks is also cause for concern. Maintaining limesinks in their natural condition with vegetative buffer zones surrounding them would aid in preventing the contamination of ground water from agrichemicals and be beneficial for wildlife.

Figure 10: *Carolina Bays and Limesinks in Georgia*

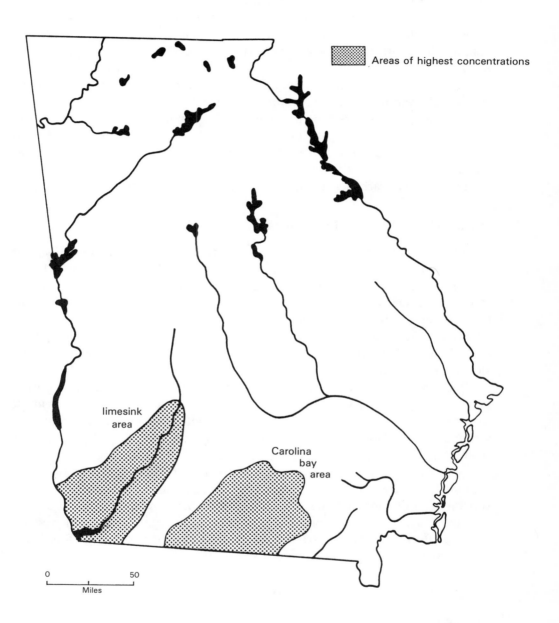

WETLANDS OF PARTICULAR VALUE

Besides the Okefenokee system, there are a number of wetlands in Georgia that are of particular value for various reasons. In the early 1970s, the now defunct Georgia Natural Areas Council identified important wetlands in the state. Incorporating this effort, the National Park Service conducted an inventory of wetlands in each state. The objective of this study was to list and classify the significant natural inland wetlands in the United States that might be suitable for registry as Natural Landmarks by the National Park Service.[34] Although the evaluation used for this inventory is broader than that used by the Fish and Wildlife Service, it appears to emphasize biological factors over other values associated with wetlands. The National Park Service's intention was to identify representative types of wetlands in each state. Table 7 presents the wetlands identified by the National Park Service as being significant in Georgia.

WETLAND TRENDS IN THE SOUTHEAST

Considerable wetland loss occurred between the mid-1950s, when the Fish and Wildlife Service conducted its first major survey of wetlands, and the mid-1970s. Nationally this amounted to a net loss of 9 million acres,[35] of which the southeastern states lost 8 million acres, more than any other region of the country.[36] States losing the most acreage of wetlands during this period include Florida, Louisiana, North Carolina, and Georgia.[37] Agricultural activities, including forestry, accounted for 87 percent of the national loss while conversion to urban and other uses accounted for 8 percent of the loss.[38]

Table 8 presents the percentage loss of wetlands during this 20-year period in the Southeast by physiographic region. Most of this loss of wetlands occurred in the Coastal Plain province. During this period, 7 percent of the estuarine wetlands in the Southeast were lost while 15 percent of the palustrine or freshwater wetlands were converted to other uses.[39]

As shown in Table 9, agriculture was the major cause of wetland conversion in all southeastern physiographic regions except along the coast. This conversion of freshwater wetlands is associated with the development of large-scale forestry and agricultural operations.[40] In the coastal region, the major wetland loss was from conversion to urban uses and the dredging and filling of wetlands for maintaining navigation channels and harbors.[41]

WETLAND TRENDS IN GEORGIA

The only wetland data comparable over time for Georgia are the Fish and Wildlife Service analyses of wetlands in the United States. Figures reported in Circular 39 indicate a mid-1950s total of wetlands in Georgia of 5,919,500 acres. These

Table 7: *Significant Wetlands in Georgia*

Name*	County	Acres	Value
Alapaha River Swamp	Irwin	100	Unusual vegetation
Alcovy River Swamp	Newton	200	Fine example of Piedmont riverine bottom
Altamaha Bottoms	Montgomery, Wheeler, Jeff Davis	12,800	Confluence of Oconee and Ocmulgee rivers, variety of wetland types, Indian history
Big Dukes Pond	Jenkins	1,100	Variety of wetland types
Little Ohoopee River Swamp	Emanuel	175	Undisturbed river swamp, gopher tortoise habitat
Lower Altamaha River Swamp (Doctortown Swamp)	McIntosh	84,000	Extensive bottomland with variety of wetland types
Middle Oconee River	Jackson	400	Fish and wildlife habitat
Murder Creek Swamp	Putnam	200	Unusual vegetation, wildlife habitat
Roundabout Swamp	Atkinson	2,000	*not available*
Sag Ponds	Floyd, Bartow	10	Six limesinks of different ages and vegetative development
Spooner Creek Swamp	Seminole	900	Undisturbed springs and natural lakes
Spring Creek Swamp	Miller	400	Boiling springs, vegetation and wildlife

Adapted from Richard H. Goodwin and William A. Niering, *Inland Wetlands of the United States,* National Park Service, 1975. *The Okefenokee Swamp is not included in this table but was included by the National Park Service in its inventory.

Table 8: *Pattern of Wetland Loss by Selected Physiographic Region, Mid-1950s — Mid-1970s*

Region	Wetland Portion of Region (Mid-1950s) (%)	Loss of Wetlands (%)
Eastern Highlands	2	2
Gulf-Atlantic Rolling Plain	8	13
Atlantic Coastal Flats	36	11
Atlantic Coastal Zone	16	3

Adapted from U.S. Office of Technology Assessment, *Wetlands: Their Use and Regulation,* 1984.

Table 9: *Percentage of Vegetated Wetland Loss to Different Uses by Selected Physiographic Region, Mid-1950s—Mid-1970s*

Region	Agriculture	Urban	Other	Water/ Nonvegetated
Eastern Highlands	38	22	5+	35
Gulf-Atlantic Rolling Plain	84	3	4+	9
Atlantic Coastal Flats	89	6	2+	3
Atlantic Coastal Zone	5	36	5	54

*Adapted from U.S. Office of Technology Assessment, *Wetlands: Their Use and Regulation,* 1984.

figures were refined but not published by the FWS in the National Wetlands Inventory to total 5,444,597 acres. In other words, the FWS overestimated wetland acreage in Georgia in the mid-1950s by nearly .5 million acres. Although these figures are considered statistically reliable at the national level, they may be less reliable at the state level.

As shown in Table 10, the figures indicate a loss of wetlands in Georgia between the mid-1950s and the mid-1970s of 146,597 acres or 2.7 percent of the refined mid-1950s wetland resources, an average loss of about 7,300 acres per year during this time period. Because of the significant increase in irrigated acres in the state since the mid-1970s, the increase in demand for forest products stimulating conversion of hardwood bottomlands to pines, and the increased rate of urban development in Georgia, the conversion of wetland acreage during the past decade (mid-1970s to mid-1980s) is likely to have been greater than during the previous 20 years.

Based on the forces identified by the FWS as affecting wetlands in the Southeast, it is likely that the bulk of the wetland loss in Georgia was in freshwater wetlands rather than salt marshes. The vast majority of wetland conversions occurred in the Coastal Plain, and between 80 percent and 90 percent

Table 10: *Wetland Trends in Georgia*

Year		Acres of Wetlands
mid-1950s*		5,444,597
mid-1970s**		5,298,000
	Total Change	− 146,597

*John M. Hefner, unpublished figures from Fish and Wildlife Service data base for National Wetlands Inventory.
**John M. Hefner and James D. Brown, ''Wetland Trends in the Southeastern United States,'' Society of Wetland Scientists, 1984.

of the conversions were caused by agricultural and forestry practices. These data do not indicate the specific types or locations of wetland conversions in the state, but they do suggest two important conclusions: (1) a substantial loss of wetlands occurred during this 20-year period, and (2) further research into the wetland situation in Georgia is needed.

SUMMARY

Georgia is one of the leading states in wetland resources, containing about 5 million acres of freshwater wetlands and salt marshes. These wetlands, however, are not evenly distributed throughout the state. The few wetlands in north Georgia are found primarily in the narrow floodplains along streams and rivers. Coastal Plain wetlands include the broad riverine bottomlands and inland wetlands such as cypress and gum ponds, Carolina bays, and limesinks. The Okefenokee Swamp is one of the largest freshwater wetlands in the country. A number of other significant wetlands have been identified in Georgia. Coastal wetlands comprise a continuum of salt, brackish, and freshwater marshes.

Between the mid-1950s and mid-1970s, the FWS data indicate a loss of 146,597 acres of wetlands in Georgia or an annual loss of about 7,300 acres. The rate of wetland conversion probably increased during the decade following the mid-1970s. Major causes of wetland conversion include drainage for agricultural and forestry production, urban and residential development, and dredging and filling for navigation purposes.

4 Wetlands and the Law

The decline of the nation's wetland resources is in part the result of our legal system's view of property and its tendency to partition into neat packages not only concepts of law but also the physical realities subject upon which the law operates. The metes and bounds of property law, however, do not conform to the realities of soil erosion, flooding, or polluted waters. Hence, the law of nuisance was developed to deter and remedy the consequences of unreasonable adjacent land uses interfering with the reasonable use of one's own property. Nuisance law was the legal system's answer to the inevitable consequences of ill-managed growth and development.

That answer, however, has proved insufficient with respect to the complexity of modern environmental problems. The more tenuous the connections between cause and effect, the less capable was the law of relegating unreasonable uses to their deserved fate. Property and nuisance laws suffer the same theoretical disadvantages in delineating the borders of private and public domain, disadvantages brought into focus by a resource such as wetlands where the traditional public ownership and control over water resources confronts the rights of private property owners on firm ground.

Unfortunately, theoretical disadvantages have turned into practical problems as our knowledge and understanding of the many interconnections pervading natural systems increases. As Chapter 2 illustrates, the ramifications of indiscriminate wetlands development can be significant, with public and private entities bearing the costs. The question inevitably arises: Are our nation's wetlands a part of the public domain or are they to be subject to the market forces of the private sector?

If the former, then the resource management policies for wetlands should be the same as those afforded rivers, lakes, and streams. If wetlands are a private property resource, then private interests will determine their fate and the consequences of their development will fall where they may. Coastal marshlands in Georgia and elsewhere are the subject of strong legislative language declaring the overriding public interest in their effective management. These declarations are in no small degree the result of ecosystem research in Georgia exploring the immense biological productivity of coastal wetlands. Likewise, inland freshwater wetlands are now the object of significant research. Thus, questions recently answered about coastal wetlands are now being answered similarly with regard to inland freshwater wetlands.

The response of the legal system has been characteristically slow. The historical antipathy with which wetlands have been viewed lingers in public attitudes and, hence, in the structure of laws and policies affecting the use of wetland environments. In contrast, recent case law and statutory law at the federal, state, and local levels are beginning to reflect an increasing realization that sensitive wetland environments are valuable resources for which public concern is amply justified and public interests are rightly asserted. Conflicting policies are a result of this contradiction, especially within the federal government, where some policies provide incentives and others impose constraints upon the conversion of wetlands to other uses.

Wetlands law is land use law, derived from two sources: legislation on the federal or state level and judicial decision. Both sources are limited in their effect by the Constitution of the United States which imposes three primary limitations on wetland and other land use laws: the "taking clause" of the Fifth Amendment, the "due process clause" of the Fifth and Fourteenth Amendments, and the "equal protection clause" embodied in the Fifteenth Amendment and equivalent state constitution provisions. These limitations raise issues of "takings" without just compensation, reasonableness, and discrimination, respectively. The application of these constitutional issues to laws regulating wetlands and other land uses merits discussion.

THE GENERAL APPROACH TO CONSTITUTIONAL DETERMINATIONS

Courts in about 20 states have considered the constitutional validity of wetland regulations. They focus first upon the general or inherent validity of the regulation and second upon the validity of the regulation as applied to the particular facts of the case. Courts in every state have sustained the general validity of wetland regulations, even where the regulations substantially reduce property values.

More frequently, the challenge is directed toward the application of the regulation to the particular facts of the case. This approach to the constitutionality of land use controls originated with two landmark decisions by the U.S. Supreme Court in the 1920s. The Court first approved the concept of zoning in *Euclid v. Amber Realty Co.*[1] and, two years later, considered *Nectow v. City of Cambridge.*[2] *Nectow* involved a zoning ordinance generally within constitutional prescriptions, but unreasonably applied to the particular property. Rather than invalidating the ordinance as a whole, the Court refused to deprive the community of the general zoning scheme and held only that the zoning plan would not apply to the property involved.

This approach to the determination of constitutionality has led to a great amount of litigation. State courts have sustained wetlands regulations as applied to inland freshwater wetlands and coastal wetlands. A county shoreland zoning ordinance, adopted pursuant to state law, was at issue in *Just v. Marinette County*[3] where the Wisconsin Supreme Court in 1972 rejected a ''taking'' challenge by stressing the government's role as trustee of public waters. The court stressed that reasonable wetland regulations fairly applied and producing widespread public benefits ''need not produce a reciprocal benefit to the owner. . . .''[4] Likewise, the Supreme Judicial Court of Massachusetts has recently upheld a highly restrictive inland wetland regulation against a ''taking'' challenge.[5] The courts of Rhode Island,[6] New York,[7] and Connecticut[8] have ruled similar wetland management efforts constitutional.

Coastal wetland laws have also received favorable treatment against challenges on constitutional grounds. Subsequent to the landmark federal court decision in *Zabel v. Tabb*[9] and similar federal holdings[10] state courts in New Jersey,[11] New Hampshire,[12] Maryland,[13] Connecticut,[14] California,[15] New York,[16] and North Carolina[17] have endorsed coastal wetland regulations. In addition, the Florida Supreme Court in 1981 in *Graham v. Estuary Properties*[18] upheld denial of a permit to destroy mangrove wetlands, adopting the Wisconsin view as expressed in *Just v. Marinette County* that ''(a)n owner of land has no absolute and unlimited right to change the essential nature of his land so as to use it for a purpose for which it is unsuited in its natural state and which injures the rights of others.''[19]

SPECIFIC CONSTITUTIONAL TESTS

Wetland regulations and ordinances have often been subjected to constitutional scrutiny. Federal, state, and local regulations are given a strong presumption of constitutionality, thus casting the burden of establishing unconstitutionality upon the opponent of the regulation.[20] This poses a significant obstacle to upsetting the general validity of a wetland regulation. The importance of the factual circumstances can outweigh the presumption of constitutionality when challenging the application of the law to individual landowners. Unconstitutionality has been asserted on the basis that it discriminates against the wetland developer, that application of the regulation is unreasonable, or that the law imposes such restrictions upon use of the wetland ''property'' that it ''takes'' private property without just compensation.

Discrimination

To avoid a successful assertion of discrimination, a regulation must give "similar treatment to landowners similarly situated" or must reasonably differentiate among landowners receiving different treatment. Such a guarantee is interpreted to arise from the Fourteenth Amendment to the U.S. Constitution.

Wetlands regulations have been challenged on grounds of discrimination in a number of cases. In *Sands Point Harbor, Inc. v. Sullivan*,[21] a New Jersey court held that the state's Wetland Act of 1970, in excluding coastal wetlands characterized by heavy industrial development from the regulatory scheme, was not discriminatory. The court found the differing conditions to afford "reasonable grounds for the differing treatment" of these coastal areas.

The Maryland Court of Appeals, in *Potomac Sand and Gravel Co. v. Governor of Maryland*,[22] held valid a dredging prohibition in the coastal area of Charles County. The Sand and Gravel Company complained that the law was discriminatory because it did not regulate inland areas. Noting the importance of coastal wetlands for fish spawning and rare plant species, the court held the distinction between coastal and inland areas constitutionally permissible.

In *J.M. Mills, Inc. v. Murphy*,[23] an inland wetland protection statute was upheld under charges that it discriminatingly failed to provide public hearings and compensation as did a similar coastal wetland law. The Rhode Island Supreme Court found a rational basis for the differing approaches.

Two cases that have held regulations discriminatory are *City of Welch v. Mitchell*[24] and *Morris County Land Improvement Co. v. Parsippany-Troy Hills Township*.[25] In *City of Welch*, a West Virginia court held as discriminatory a local floodplain ordinance that regulated development on one side of a stream and not the other. A conservancy zone in *Morris County* was invalid in part because it discriminated between upstream and downstream landowners.

Reasonableness

The reasonableness requirement of the Fourteenth Amendment's due process clause demands that the means by which a subject is regulated must be reasonably related to the ends sought to be achieved. Thus, courts have invalidated floodplain regulations applicable to areas with no evidence of flooding;[26] regulations requiring enclosed drainage systems in circumstances where open drainage systems were more appropriate;[27] and pollution control requirements where there was little threat of pollution.[28] When regulations impose restrictions on the uses of private land, courts are especially demanding of a strong relationship between ends and means. The reasonableness of wetland regulations arises in a number of contexts.

Regulations Based upon Inadequate Data

Regulations based upon inadequate data will lack a reasonable relationship to regulatory objectives. Kusler[29] discusses the necessary considerations:

> At a minimum, statutory data gathering and mapping requirements must be followed. If there are no statutory requirements, the issue of reasonableness depends not only upon the quality and quantity of data, but also upon the specific nature of the regulations based upon these data, the impact of the regulations upon private property owners, and the data refinement procedures available during administration of regulations. Soil maps may be sufficient for wetland definition in rural environments where property values are relatively low and the impact of regulations upon landowners is minimal, but soil maps may be less acceptable for high value urban areas.

Landowning challengers to wetland legislation often contest the reasonableness of the state or local government's wetland map. In the *Just*[30] case, the county's use of U.S. Geological Survey topographic maps combined with written criteria applied on a case-by-case basis through field surveys was upheld by the Wisconsin Supreme Court. The New Jersey Supreme Court, in *Loveladies Property Owners Ass'n, Inc. v. Rabb,*[31] held mapping of wetlands to be a prerequisite to requiring permits for regulated landowners. In *State v. Capuano Bros., Inc.,*[32] the Rhode Island Supreme Court upheld the use of air photos to indicate wetlands in the 50-year floodplain, the area that can statistically be expected to be flooded once in a 50-year period. Floodplain maps were upheld in *A.H. Smith Sand & Gravel Co. v. Dept. of Water Resources*[33] although the Maryland Supreme Court required that the maps be modified to reflect recent flood data.

Regulation of Wetland Area Subzones

Although no court has considered the issue, delimiting subzones within mapped wetland areas may be advisable. This would permit degrees of restrictions where substantial variations exist in flood hazard, pollution potential, wildlife value, and other wetland values, especially in areas of high property value.[34] The courts of New Jersey[35] and Connecticut[36] have found ''takings'' of private property subjected to highly restrictive regulations applicable to the entire wetland or floodplain area.

Regulations Accounting for Cumulative Impacts

As mentioned in Chapter 3, the cumulative impacts of multiple projects in a wetland area may produce detrimental effects beyond the reach of requiring individual project permits. The Supreme Court of Wisconsin, in upholding denial of a permit to maintain a breakwater, observed:[37]

> A little fill here and there may seem to be nothing to become excited about. But one fill, though comparatively inconsequential, may lead to another,

and before long a great body of water may be eaten away until it may no longer exist. Our navigable waters are a precious natural heritage; once gone, they disappear forever.

The California Supreme Court sustained regulations restricting fill operations in San Francisco Bay based in part upon arguments of cumulative impact.[38] Although arguments of cumulative impact were presented to the courts in *National Land & Investment Co. v. Kohn*[39] in Pennsylvania and *Christine Bldg. Co. v. City of Troy*[40] in Michigan, evidence of the anticipated development was deemed insufficient to justify the land use restrictions. Although insufficient in these particular cases, cumulative impacts are not constitutionally impermissible but like any regulation must reasonably relate to the regulatory objectives sought to be achieved.

The Taking Issue

The constitutional "taking" issue is one of the thorniest of legal thickets and there are many ways to conceptualize the problems. Wetland regulation has exposed these difficulties as well as any regulatory scheme. A variety of tests have evolved over the years with little direction from the U.S. Supreme Court.

Determinations of takings are often concluded from proof of discriminatory effect, unreasonableness, and failure to comply with other constitutional requirements. The taking regulation is usually one of permanent and highly restrictive effect. Almost all cases in which a taking is found have involved regulations that prevented all development in the wetland area, regardless of whether hazards, nuisances, or the absence of practical use remained. Over the years a balancing test has evolved where public interests in the regulation are pitted against the impact on private property owners. The courts also apply several specific tests which qualify the balancing process.

Physical Invasion

When the government physically enters upon the property of a private landowner is the clearest of all instances of takings. Flooding of private property by the federal government's construction of a dam was found to be a taking by the U.S. Supreme Court in *Pumpbelly v. Green Bay Company.*[41] The physical invasion has little application to wetland regulations since a physical invasion test of the wetland property is usually not involved.

Diminution in Value

The classic "diminution in value" test was formulated by Chief Justice Holmes of the U.S. Supreme Court in *Pennsylvania Coal Co. v. Mahon,* when he declared that

> One fact for consideration . . . is the extent of the diminution. When it reaches
> a certain magnitude, in most if not all cases there must be an exercise of
> eminent domain and compensation to sustain the act. So the question
> depends upon the particular facts.[42]

Indeed, the facts of each case are controlling when the diminution in value test
is applied, and consequently the test has little predictive value. The Supreme
Court reiterated the determinative nature of the facts but reduced the importance
of the test in *Goldblatt v. Town of Hempstead*[43] where it held that ''[t]here is
no set formula to determine where regulation ends and taking begins. Although
a comparison of values before and after is relevant . . . it is by no means conclu-
sive.'' The concept of diminution in value has been cited in many wetland cases
but has not been widely applied as a final measure of an unconstitutional taking.[44]

Police Power versus Eminent Domain

The validity of any law passed pursuant to the state's police power rests on
the state's duty to protect the public health, safety, morals, and general welfare.
The power of eminent domain is invoked by the government to acquire property for a needed public use. The difference is between the prevention of a
public harm and the creation of a public benefit. A ''taking'' will be found
if the regulations require the landowners to confer an uncompensated benefit
to the public.[45] Protection of public safety is one of government's most sacred
functions and courts generally allow great latitude to the legislative body; in
the land use context, judicial scrutiny is more pronounced. The judicial search
for the underlying regulatory objective is determinative under this test. In
wetlands cases, two regulatory objectives—protection of aesthetics and maintenance of status quo until public purchase is possible—have not passed muster.
Valid exercises of the police power, however, have been found in the following
regulatory objectives: protection of public health and safety, prevention of
nuisances, protection of wildlife and fisheries, prevention of flood damage, water
pollution control, and protection of water supply.

Protection of aesthetics. Although traditionally unaccepted as a proper objective of the state's police power, aesthetics are now recognized as a valid primary
objective in some states and a valid secondary objective in all states, effectively adding weight to primary police power goals such as flood and water
quality protection. Judicial acceptance of aesthetics under the police power is
largely due to their positive relation to the tax base.[46]

Maintenance of status quo until public purchase is possible. Attempts to
zone or otherwise restrict land use for the purpose of holding land open until
public purchase have often been held invalid.[47] Such circumstances are to be
distinguished from lands properly regulated yet identified for long-term public
purchase.

Protection of public health and safety. Without exception, courts have held valid any regulation protecting public health and safety. The general rule, as stated by the Supreme Court in *Queenside Hills Realty Co. v. Saxl,* is that such regulations may steer "the most conservative course which science and engineering offer."[48]

Prevention of nuisances. States have inherent power to prohibit "noxious uses" of property[49] and may, for objectives of public health and safety,[50] regulate even existing uses of property out of existence.[51] Applying the rule in *Filister v. City of Minneapolis,*[52] the Minnesota Supreme Court sustained a single-family residential classification for a wetland area surrounded by residences in part because of the nuisance-like effect of an apartment complex in the low-density surroundings.

Protection of wildlife and fisheries. Numerous wetland cases have recognized the proper role of the police power to protect fish and wildlife resources. The Fifth Circuit Court of Appeals in *Zabel v. Tabb*[53] affirmed this principle in upholding a dredging permit denial by the U.S. Army Corps of Engineers in a Florida mangrove area. The court recognized that, as far as the United States' interests were concerned, ". . .the destruction of fish and wildlife in our estuarine waters does have a substantial, and in some areas a devastating effect on interstate commerce."[54] State interests in fish and wildlife protection were acknowledged by the Maryland Supreme Court in *Potomac Sand & Gravel Co. v. Governor of Maryland.*[55] Endorsing a statute prohibiting dredging the tidal waters and marshlands of Charles County, the court showed rare insight into the biological realities behind this police power objective:

> . . .the sites in question support such species of fish as herring, American shad, hickory shad, striped bass, white perch and eel perch, among others. These fish are sources for commercial fishing and sport fishing throughout Maryland. The testimony is undisputed that dredging would irreparably destroy the immediate marsh habitat, converting it into a deep-water habitat. Consequently, those anadromous fish which spawn in shallow waters and which instinctively return each year to the same spawning areas would be deprived of such spawning areas with a concomitant loss of the benefits of their reproductive process. Dredging increases turbidity. . .[which] reduces the amount of sunlight. . .reach[ing] aquatic plants, which, through photosynthesis, produce oxygen for fish. The plants are a food source for fish which would be reduced both due to the failure of plants to reproduce and by the smothering of plants by dirt particles.
>
> [W]ildlife. . .would be frightened away by dredging noises as well as driven away by a loss of an accessible food supply. [D]ucks would be unable to readily retrieve their food fifty feet below the surface.

The court went on to hold the regulation to be a valid exercise of police power authority. Police power protection of fish and wildlife values is also recognized in other states.[56]

Prevention of flood damage. Flood protection by police power regulation of land use is widely recognized by the courts. In *Turnpike Realty Co. v. Town of Dedham*,[57] the Massachusetts Supreme Judicial Court noted that the "general necessity of floodplain zoning to reduce the damage to life and property caused by flooding is unquestionable."[58]

Water pollution control. The control of water pollution, as with flood protection, is a police power concern closely related to the strongly endorsed objective of protecting the public health and safety. Thus, judicial recognition of the links between wetland protection and water pollution control and flood damage is important to the validity of regulatory management efforts. Although the Maine Supreme Court in *State v. Johnson*[59] held invalid a fill restriction in a coastal wetland, the court noted that considerations of health and pollution could well support validity of the law in those areas of concern.[60] Judicial recognition of the link between wetlands and water quality was established by the Wisconsin Supreme Court in *Just v. Marinette County*:[61]

> What makes this case different from most condemnation or police power zoning cases is the interrelationship of the wetlands, the swamps and the natural environment of shorelands to the purity of the water and to natural resources as navigation, fishing, and scenic beauty. Swamps and wetlands were once considered wasteland, undesirable, and not picturesque...but as the people became more sophisticated, an appreciation was acquired that swamps and wetlands serve a vital role in nature, and are essential to the purity of the water in our lakes and streams. Swamps and wetlands are a necessary part of the ecological creation....

Cases involving the validity of dredge and fill regulations under section 404 of the Clean Water Act have also noted the relationship between the regulations and pollution.

Protection of water supply. Public water supplies are protectable by means of police power regulation. The U.S. Supreme Court in *Perley v. North Carolina*[62] upheld a state statute prohibiting private forestry operations within 400 feet of city watersheds held for water supply purposes. The Massachusetts Supreme Judicial Court acted similarly in *Lovequist v. Conservation Commission of the Town of Dennis*[63] by upholding regulations protecting ground water supplies.

Denial of All Practical Use

The fourth and most common constitutional test applied by the courts in wetland cases looks to the remaining uses of land under regulation. Restrictions that deny all ''practical'' or ''reasonable'' uses are said to take the property in question without just compensation. A distinction between a denial of all ''practical'' use and all ''reasonable'' use may be important in certain circumstances. Although highly restrictive regulations for a coastal wetland subject to severe flood hazards may, for marinas, prevent all practical uses, the unreasonableness of any use under such circumstances does not deny the owner the reasonable use of his land.[64] The practical use rule has several important qualifications:

Public safety and nuisance. Denying a landowner all practical uses of his land does not impede the effect of regulations for the protection of public safety or preventing serious conflicts between adjacent properties. Public safety regulations are given a special presumption of constitutionality. Threats to safety from open excavations of sand and gravel justified the U.S. Supreme Court's validation of an ordinance preventing all economic use of the property in *Goldblatt v. Town of Hempstead.*[65]

In the flood hazard context, tight controls over development have been upheld. In *Spiegle v. Borough of Beach Haven,*[66] the New Jersey Supreme Court sustained a beach development setback line imposed by local ordinance. The court emphasized that the landowner had failed to show that the certain hazards of building in the area would allow him any beneficial economic use of which he could be deprived.[67] The U.S. Supreme Court, in *Mugler v. Kansas,*[68] propounded the traditional reasoning behind this qualification to the rule:[69]

> The exercise of the police power by the destruction of property which is itself a public nuisance, or the prohibition of its use in a particular way, whereby its value becomes depreciated, is very different from taking property for public use, or from depriving a person of his property without due process of law. In the one case, a nuisance only is abated; in the other, unoffending property is taken away from an innocent owner.

Availability of special permits. Special permits essentially bend regulations to the particular factual circumstances of the applicant. Thus, the regulation does not, at least on its face, deny the landowner all practical land uses. For example, a permit denial under the state floodway protection law was upheld by the Connecticut Supreme Court in *Vartelas v. Water Resources Commission.*[70] Denial of a permit for one proposed use was held not to be equivalent to a denial of all possible uses, the applicant's remedy being to submit another permit application. Similarly, ordinances authorizing special exceptions were upheld in part for that reason in the *Just* case[71] and in *Turnpike Realty Co.*[72]

Regulations affecting a portion of the property. Where practical uses can be made of other portions of the same property, takings are less likely to be found. In the important 1978 case of *Penn Central Transportation Co. v. New York City,*[73] the U.S. Supreme Court clearly enunciated the principle:

"Taking" jurisprudence does not divide a single parcel into discrete segments and attempt to determine whether rights in a particular segment have been entirely abrogated. In deciding whether a particular government action has effected a taking, this Court focuses rather both on the character of the action and on the nature and extent of the interference with rights in the parcel as a whole. . . .

Citing *Penn Central,* the Court of Claims upheld denials of section 404 permits for Florida mangrove wetlands.

Filling restrictions were also upheld by the New Jersey Supreme Court in *American Dredging Co. v. N.J. Department of Environmental Protection.*[74] The regulation was affecting 80 out of 2,500 acres owned by the company, and the court factored the impact accordingly.

Purchase with knowledge. Purchasing a parcel of land with knowledge of the restrictions to which it is subject further qualifies the denial of all practical use. Such circumstances were significant in the South Dakota Supreme Court ruling in *Chokecherry Hills Estates Inc. v. Devel County.*[75] The court concluded that ". . . the evidence paints a picture of [this landowner] taking a gamble that he could succeed in changing the existing zoning law so that he could realize a higher profit."[76]

Public rights in navigable waters. The rule of practical use, and indeed the entire taking analysis, yields to the federal navigation servitude and the public trust doctrine. The navigation servitude derives from the commerce power under the Constitution whereas the public trust derives from state interests in the tidelands of the coasts. Under the navigational servitude, the federal government can prevent or take the use of a navigable river without regard to title under state law.[77] Although traditionally limited to waters and lands within the high water mark of public waters,[78] the public trust doctrine has been more broadly applied in recent years.[79] The New Hampshire Supreme Court, in *Sibson v. State* stated that

> [R]ights of littoral landowners on public waters are always subject to the paramount right of the State to control them reasonably in the interests of navigation, fishing, and other public purposes.[80]

The effect of either doctrine is to erect a barrier to judicial consideration of a taking claim, the practical result of which is a rule of "no compensation."

SUMMARY OF LEGAL IMPLICATIONS

The courts have been heavily involved in resolving conflicts between public interests in wetlands and private "land" use prerogatives. Courts have tended to uphold regulations that treat similarly those that are similarly situated (nondiscriminatory) and regulations that provide means logically related to the ends sought to be achieved (reasonableness). But if nondiscriminatory and reasonable regulations deprive the private landowner of the practical use of his land, those regulations are likely to be declared "takings" unless the law pursues valid police power objectives. Wetland legislation that legitimately seeks to protect the public health, safety, and welfare will always be upheld.

5 Federal, State, and Local Wetland Programs

Early congressional action exemplified the reigning view of the mid-1800s that wetlands were valuable only to the extent agricultural production could supplant them. The Swamp Land Acts of 1849, 1850, and 1860 granted to 15 states[1] all swamp and overflow lands within their borders. States were to reclaim these wetlands by constructing levees and drains for the purposes of lessening flood damage, eliminating mosquito-breeding swamps, and encouraging settlement and agricultural development.[2] By 1954, almost 65 million acres of wetlands had been transferred from the federal government. Nearly all the transferred wetlands are now in private ownership and, pursuant to several federal programs, are being bought and leased at considerable cost to federal taxpayers.[3] Georgia and the other 12 original states retained all unsold land within their boundaries when the federal government was first organized.

FEDERAL WETLAND PROGRAMS

Wetland values began to receive recognition with the 1956 Fish Wildlife Service analysis of wetlands when contradicting federal policies began to attract public and congressional attention. In 1962, concern for waterfowl habitat prompted Congress to eliminate the Agricultural Conservation Program's cost-sharing and technical assistance for wetland drainage in Minnesota, North Dakota, and South Dakota if the secretary of the interior found material threats to wildlife preservation. Between 1942 and 1980, almost 57 million acres of wet farmland, including some wetlands, were drained under this program.

Currently, federal involvement with wetland resources occurs under the auspices of several types of programs, addressing such areas as regulatory permitting, state and local assistance, federal land management, wetland research, and agricultural conversion policies.[4] Each of these federal programs was modified by President Carter's two executive orders establishing wetland protection and flood plain management as the official policy of all federal agencies.

Federal Policy

Executive Order 11990[5] was promulgated in May 1977 and mandates that all federal agencies in pursuing their responsibilities "take action to minimize the destruction, loss or degradation of wetlands, and to preserve and enhance the natural and beneficial values of wetlands. . . ." Agencies are specifically directed to avoid assisting or undertaking new construction in wetlands unless there is no practical alternative. The agencies must also provide all practical measures to minimize harm to wetlands in the action taken, and consider a proposal's effect on the survival and quality of the wetland area.

Indirect protection of wetland resources was provided by President Carter's Executive Order 11988,[6] Flood Plain Management. The order requires each federal agency to avoid direct or indirect support of flood plain development wherever there is a practical alternative.

Executive Orders 11990 and 11988 apply to federal activities such as construction projects, acquisition and disposal of lands, and grants-in-aid and technical assistance to states for land and water planning and the building of roads, sewers, and water supply systems. They do not apply to federal permitting or licensing activity on private property.[7]

Regulatory Permitting Programs

The federal government currently regulates wetland activities under two inter-related permit programs, each administered by the Army Corps of Engineers.

Rivers and Harbors Act of 1899

Permits are required under the Rivers and Harbors Act of 1899 for the dredging, filling, or obstruction of "navigable waters," a term interpreted by the Corps to exclude wetlands above the mean high water mark. In 1968, however, the Corps responded to increased public concern over environmental protection by expanding its permit evaluation criteria to include considerations of effects on "navigation, fish and wildlife, conservation, pollution, aesthetics, ecology and the general public interest."[8] As previously discussed, one result of this action was the landmark decision by the U.S. Fifth Circuit Court of Appeals in the case of *Zabel v. Tabb*,[9] upholding the denial of a permit to fill 11 acres of a mangrove swamp solely on the grounds of environmental damage. Corps jurisdiction, however, remained fixed at the mean high water mark and construction in wetlands outside commercially navigable waters was left unregulated.

Clean Water Act—Section 404

The second permit program under which the Corps of Engineers regulates wetland activities was established by the 1972 amendments to the Federal Water Pollution Control Act (FWPCA), and actually incorporates the Rivers and

Harbors Act permits by reference.[10] Section 404 of the FWPCA (and the modern Section 404 of the Clean Water Act) requires permits to be obtained for discharges of dredged and fill materials into the "waters of the United States."

Corps regulatory framework. To understand the modern jurisdictional scope of this mandate it is important to examine the historical context in which it evolved. The first Corps regulations narrowly interpreted this language to include only traditionally navigable waters, until a U.S. District Court held otherwise. The court, in *Natural Resources Defense Council v. Callaway,*[11] determined the 1972 language to have broadened the permit program to include all waters including wetlands.

To comply with the court's order, the Corps in 1975 broadened its jurisdiction to include not only traditionally navigable waters but also[12]

1. artificially created channels connected to navigable waters;
2. tributaries to navigable waters up to their headwaters;
3. nonnavigable interstate waters up to their headwaters;
4. intrastate waters up to their headwaters that are used for interstate commerce;
5. wetlands adjacent to such waters; and
6. wetlands that are located above the high mean water mark but are adjacent to interstate waters or their tributaries.

The new regulations defined "headwaters" of a stream to be those above which the flow is normally less than five cubic feet per second. For the first time, Corps regulations recognized and defined "freshwater wetlands" as areas "periodically inundated" and "normally characterized by the prevalance of vegetation that requires saturated soil conditions for growth and reproduction."[13]

The Corps' broad assertion of jurisdiction over waters not actually navigable in fact and adjacent wetlands engendered considerable congressional opposition in 1977. Debate on proposals to narrow the definition of "navigable waters" centered largely on the issue of wetlands preservation.[14] The jurisdictional scope of section 404 was, however, retained and the 1977 amendments statutorily authorized regulatory control over adjacent wetlands.[15]

Subsequent interpretations of this jurisdictional mandate by the Corps have led to alterations in the regulatory scope of 404 permitting. Corps regulations now recognize "wetlands" as "areas that are inundated or saturated by surface water or ground water at a frequency and duration sufficient to support, and that under normal circumstances do support, a prevalance of vegetation typically adapted for life in saturated soil conditions."[16] Neither periodic inundations[17] nor vegetation that requires saturated soil conditions[18] are necessary for the determination that an area is a wetland.

Although jurisdiction was expanded to regulate development in many of the nation's wetlands, the 1977 Clean Water Act restricted wetlands protection in two important ways:[19]

1. *Exemptions* from 404 permits were allowed for
   a. normal farming, silvicultural,...and ranching activities...; minor drainage; harvesting for the production of food, fiber, and forest products; or upland soil and water conservation practices;
   b. maintenance... of currently serviceable structures such as dikes, dams, levees, groins, riprap,...breakwaters, causeways, bridge abutments or approaches, and transportation structures;
   c. construction or maintenance of farm or stock ponds or irrigation ditches, or the maintenance of drainage ditches;
   d. construction of temporary sedimentation basins on a construction site, but excluding placement of fill material into navigable waters;
   e. construction or maintenance of farm or forest roads, or temporary roads for moving mining equipment, where such roads are constructed and maintained in accordance with best management practices...;
   f. congressionally approved projects that have filed an environmental impactment statement (EIS).
2. *Categorized permitting* whereby certain activities deemed by the Corps to have minor impacts on waters of the United States are not subject to the more closely scrutinized procedures for individual permits. These permits are characterized as either "nationwide" or "regional" permits.

The potential impact of exemptions for "normal" farming and other activities is mitigated by Section 404(f)(2) of the Clean Water Act (CWA), which nevertheless requires permits if the activity will bring an area of navigable waters into a use to which it was not previously subject. Wetlands protection was affected by the Corps' regulatory decision to allow categories of nationwide permits for wetlands adjacent to the "headwaters" of nontidal streams and for small lakes and isolated wetlands less than 10 acres in size. Subsequent 1982 and 1983 regulations expanded these exemptions from individualized permitting to include any isolated wetland regardless of size. A lawsuit by the National Wildlife Federation and others, however, resulted in a 1984 settlement agreement requiring the Corps to modify its regulations to require notification by permit applicants before performing activities that will cause loss or modification of more than one acre of wetland. The Corps then has 20 days to impose conditions on the project. The settlement also requires activities affecting 10 acres or more of wetland to obtain an individual permit.[20]

Other recent changes in the Corps' regulatory framework include redefinition of the term "adjacent" to further require that regulated wetlands have "a reasonably perceptible surface or subsurface hydrologic connection to waters of the United States.'' [21] The 1983 changes also allow minor discharges into wetlands upon receipt from the Corps of a "letter of permission" rather than a permit. In addition, the new regulations explicitly shift the burden of proof to the federal government such that 404 permit applications are now accepted unless the Corps affirmatively demonstrates conditions of unacceptability. Thus, the Corps of Engineers has consistently narrowed the jurisdictional reach of the 404 program, more so since 1982.

Role of other agencies. Implementation of the 404 program involves three other federal agencies in addition to the limited state involvement. The Environmental Protection Agency (EPA), the National Marine Fisheries Service (NMFS), and the Fish Wildlife Service review permit applications and provide comments and recommendations on whether permits should be issued by the Corps. EPA has veto authority over permits involving disposal sites if impacts are considered unacceptable. EPA also develops criteria for discharges and state assumption of the 404 program.

States have authority under this program to veto permit applications by denying certification through section 401 of the CWA and may administer portions of the 404 program if they meet EPA criteria. Under the law, states can assume the 404 permit issuing authority only in nonnavigable waters; the Corps maintains permit issuing authority in wetlands directly adjacent to navigable streams. Because states have only partial permit-issuing authority, together with a lack of funds to finance this activity and unacceptable regulatory requirements, few states have pursued this permitting authority.[22] As of this time, Michigan is the only state to apply for authority to assume the 404 program; its application is pending. Twelve states are evaluating the possibility of assuming 404 responsibilities and four have assumed partial responsibility for the program on a trial basis. It appears that most states neither have the capability nor the desire to pursue such authority without additional financial assistance from the federal government.

Effectiveness of the 404 program. In most areas of the nation, section 404 of the CWA is the only government program managing the development of wetland environments. Because of enforcement inadequacies and the program's limited scope, section 404 has not been entirely effective at controlling wetland alterations.

Generally, the 404 program suffers from a lack of certainty regarding the scope of both its purpose and its jurisdiction. Although the Corps of Engineers views its primary 404 function as one of protecting water quality, the EPA, the FWS and the NMFS consider habitat and other wetland values to fall within the mandate of the CWA.[23]

The jurisdictional reach of the 404 program has been an issue hotly debated for many years. Judicial interpretations have consistently expanded the scope of Corps responsibility. A major limitation with regard to wetlands jurisdiction, however, has not been an issue of dispute. That limitation interposes 404 permit review only for the *discharge* of dredge or fill material into wetland environments. Projects converting wetlands by other means are not regulated by the Corps or by anyone else in Georgia. Thus, drainage, dredging and excavation, vegetation removal, and upland activities affecting wetlands do not come within the Corps' jurisdiction unless removed materials are discharged back into the wetland area.

Even for wetland activities involving the discharge of dredge or fill material, unless that wetland is adjacent to a *tidal* river only the few application and reporting requirements of regional or nationwide permits will apply. Thus, the 404 program has limited regulatory control over wetlands adjacent to nontidal rivers, wetlands adjacent to stream "headwaters" and natural lakes under 10 acres, and isolated wetlands. Further restricting the reach of 404 jurisdiction are the express exemptions adopted in the 1977 amendments to the CWA.

For those wetlands falling within the scope of the Corps' 404 jurisdiction, inadequate enforcement of regulations contributes to the ineffectiveness of the program. The Corps lacks adequate resources to effectively regulate activities in all waters of the United States.[24] This fact has contributed to the Corps' intent (congressionally authorized in 1977) to regulate many wetland areas with the nationwide or regional permits mentioned above.

The 404 program is also beset with several administrative problems limiting the effectiveness of regulation. One such problem involves significant variations in the way different Corps districts implement key elements of the program. For example, the regulation of agricultural conversions by drainage involving the discharge of fill from ditching operations is accomplished by means of individual permits in some districts and by regional or nationwide permits in other districts. Other such conversions are not regulated at all due to failure of Corps administration and inadequate enforcement.[25] Generally, administrative and enforcement priorities of each Corps district reflect the political realities of the state in which it is located.

Another example of administrative limitations involves present Corps policy of not regulating the clearing of bottom lands, many of which are found in Georgia. After a recent order by the Fifth Circuit Court of Appeals extending jurisdiction over such clearing operations in Louisiana,[26] the Corps has followed the questionable policy of not appealing the decision, apparently to avoid having to regulate similar clearing operations beyond that portion of Louisiana affected by the court's order. A U.S. Supreme Court affirmance of the Fifth Circuit order would require nationwide jurisdiction over bottomland wetlands. Other administrative problems involve the lack of coordination among some Corps districts and other federal and state agencies, inadequate public awareness efforts, and the low priority given to monitoring and enforcing the 404 program.[27]

Federal Assistance to States and Localities

Various federal statutes and policies provide assistance to states and localities for the protection of wetland resources. Other than the CWA's offer of state control over portions of the 404 permit program, such nonregulatory possibilities include several forms of technical and financial assistance, grants-in-aid, and the funding of wetland-related research. Many of these measures operate as incentives to states in the form of federal dollars or by conforming federal projects to state and local regulations. Several of the assistance measures operate to encourage wetland alterations.

Technical Assistance

Localities may opt for several forms of technical assistance in developing and implementing programs for wetland protection or broader land and water management programs incorporating wetland protection components.

Fish and Wildlife Service. The 1977 amendments to the CWA provide for assistance by the Fish Wildlife Service in developing regulatory programs for the discharge of dredged and fill material into wetlands adjacent to waters of the United States. This section of the CWA, section 208, also is the statutory authorization for the FWS National Wetlands Inventory (Chapter 2). The inventory can be especially useful to state and local governments for land use planning and zoning purposes.

U.S. Department of Agriculture. The U.S. Department of Agriculture (USDA) and the Soil Conservation Service (SCS) provide technical assistance to states, local governments, and private landowners in several aspects of resource conservation. The USDA's Agricultural Conservation Program (ACP) provides farmers up to 80 percent of construction costs for a variety of conservation practices. The ACP provides funding for several farming practices, such as irrigation reservoir and land leveling, that indirectly give rise to wetland conversions. Indeed, the USDA actively assisted wetland drainage with technical information and cost sharing until 1977. From 1942 to 1980, the ACP program assisted the drainage of nearly 57 million acres of wet farmland, including some wetlands.[28] The SCS may also provide direct technical assistance for wetland drainage. In 1975, however, the SCS made a major shift in wetlands policy by the issuance of Conservation Planning Memorandum 15 which eliminated technical and financial assistance for draining or otherwise altering wetlands of all but two types (seasonally flooded basins, flats and fresh meadows).[29] Recently, SCS has asserted the need for a "margin of flexibility" for such technical assistance.[30] "[M]inor alterations of types 1 through 20 [may receive assistance] if the net result is equivalent or greater habitat values."[31] The Office of Technology Assessment concludes that the implementation of the cost-sharing programs is increasingly responsive to policies to protect remaining wetlands.[32]

Army Corps of Engineers. States and localities may also receive floodplain management technical services from the Army Corps of Engineers. Assistance under the Corps' floodplain management program is important to wetlands protection and management in that the program stresses non-structural approaches (such as floodplain regulations) in controlling flood losses.

Financial Assistance

Federal incentives to convert wetlands to other uses are in several instances provided by direct financial assistance. Subsidized insurance policies and the federal income tax code are the primary vehicles by which conversion incentives are implemented.

Subsidized flood insurance. The National Flood Insurance Program (NFIP) was created in 1968 in response to mounting federal expenditures in disaster relief and increasing evidence that structural flood control measures could not provide adequate protection. The NFIP provides federal financial assistance in the form of subsidized flood insurance (up to 90 percent federal subsidy) to homeowners and businesses in flood-prone areas where insurers are often unwilling to accept the risk. To come under the program, state and local governments must establish land use controls over floodplain development by zoning, subdivision regulations, building codes, or other means. No technical assistance is available to local governments qualifying for coverage.

Wetlands may receive a considerable degree of protection from the NFIP,[33] especially riverine wetlands that assist in reducing flood damage. Although rules are now in force discouraging building in areas of known flood risk and lessening the impacts of developments that do take place,[34] the program indirectly encourages wetland degradation and loss by underwriting development risks in the floodplain.

More than 17,000 communities nationwide have adopted or have indicated an intent to adopt floodplain regulations pursuant to the NFIP.[35] Georgia has 445 communities with mapped flood-prone areas.[36]

Federal income tax incentives. The federal tax code contains several provisions allowing farmers to shift a portion of the investment costs of wetland conversion to the general taxpayer. Tax incentives for agricultural conversion include deductions from taxable income for land-clearing costs of up to $5,000 or 25 percent of taxable income, whichever is less; deductions of up to 25 percent of gross farm income for drainage expenses (any excess expenses are deductible in subsequent years); investment tax credits for 10 percent of drainage tile installation costs; depreciation deductions on all capital investments necessary to clearing and drainage operations; and deductions for interest payments. As income rises, the value of the tax incentives generally increases.[37]

Other federal financial assistance programs operate to encourage wetland conversions. Farmers Home Administration loans can provide low interest rate financing of conversion activities. Although Executive Orders 11990 and 11988 are applicable, the broad discretion allowed state and local decision makers may cancel their protective policies.[38] Federal disaster payments and crop insurance have also subsidized agriculture in high risk flood-prone areas such as wetlands.

A significant change in federal policy occurred, however, with the passage of the 1985 omnibus farm bill (H.R. 2100). Included in this bill was a wetlands protection provision known as the "swampbuster" program. Under this section, farm program benefits would be lost by any person who converts wetland to use for agricultural commodities produced by cultivating the soil. The bill defines "converting" wetland to include draining, dredging, filling, leveling or otherwise treating the land to make it suitable for cultivation.

Grants-in-aid

State, local, and private wetland protection efforts are supported by several categories of federal grants-in-aid programs. These include programs for wetlands acquisition, land and water use planning, wetlands regulation, and grants-in-aid for research and training. Grants-in-aid for state and local acquisition of wetlands are administered by three principal programs.

Pittman-Robertson funds. The first of these is the Federal Aid to Wildlife Restoration Act,[39] commonly known as the Pittman-Robertson Act, which provides funds for wildlife habitat acquisition. Grants are administered by the FWS and are available for up to 75 percent of project costs. An 11 percent excise tax on the sale of firearms and ammunition is the source of this funding. Nationwide, over 1.5 million acres of wetland waterfowl habitat have been acquired. Pittman-Robertson funds are collected by the Department of the Interior and apportioned among the states.

Georgia's Game and Fish Division has budgeted an average of about $2 million in Pittman-Robertson funds annually over the last five years. Habitat acquisition spending varies from year to year but generally consumes only a small portion of the budgeted amount. Wetland areas are incidentally acquired when purchasing wildlife habitat; specifically, the division's last two purchases have included riverine wetland areas on the Ocmulgee and Oconee rivers in Middle Georgia.[40]

Dingell-Johnson funds. A second funding source for wetland acquisition is the Federal Aid in Fish Restoration Act,[41] commonly known as the Dingell-Johnson Act, which addresses its concern to projects involving fish habitat in a manner parallel to that of the Pittman-Robertson Act. These funds can be used to acquire wetland habitat associated with fish restoration and management projects.[42]

Georgia's Game and Fish Division has budgeted an average of $541,000 per year over the last five years in Dingell-Johnson funds; an additional amount averaging about $60,000 annually over the last five years has been allotted to the Department of Natural Resources Coastal Resources Division for saltwater fishing programs.[43] Most of the expenditures in Georgia are for management-applied research and survey projects; few if any of these funds have been used to acquire critical habitat areas such as wetlands. Congress has directed an expansion of this program for fiscal year 1986 such that Georgia officials anticipate a 1986 budget of $1.5 million to $2.0 million dollars.[44]

Coastal Zone Management funds. The Coastal Zone Management Act (CZMA) is a third source of funding for wetland acquisition. The program is administered by the National Oceanic and Atmospheric Administration's Office of Coastal Zone Management, which sets guidelines and provides funding for states contingent upon preparation and enforcement of a state program. Specific provisions provide for wetland impact considerations and annual reviews of program implementations. The CZMA provides grants-in-aid of up to $6 million per year on a 50-50 basis to acquire estuarine sanctuaries for preservation as scientific, cultural, or recreational areas. An example of a wetland sanctuary acquired under the CZMA is 6,150 acres of Georgia's Sapelo Island. Pittman-Robertson funds assisted in this purchase. Since Georgia withdrew from the federal Coastal Zone Management program in 1979, however, these funds are no longer available for use in the state.

Other federal programs exist that may fund wetland protection or acquisition. The Land and Water Conservation Fund Act of 1965 has provided funds to the FWS for expansion of the National Wildlife Refuge System, a significant portion of which includes wetland environments, and to the National Park Service for land purchases. The USDA administers the Water Bank Program, which concentrates on the purchase of easements on wetland areas in the prairie pothole region of the northern Midwest. Funds allocated to states pursuant to CWA section 208 may also be used for programs to control non-point source pollution which may significantly impact wetland environments.

Wetland Research Programs

Research in wetland areas is scattered among several federal agencies and programs. The Corps of Engineers is the only federal agency that has a program specifically addressing wetland research. The Corps' Waterways Experiment Station is carrying out a five-year program that began in 1982 to develop improved techniques for defining and evaluating wetlands and to assemble a data base of regional literature on wetland studies.[45]

The FWS central research program allocates 5 to 7 percent of its total budget for wetland research. The FWS research involves the development of research bibliographies and the evaluation of wetland assessment techniques, wastewater disposal impacts, and mapping technologies. The NMFS is also active in wetlands research. About one-half of its $6 million habitat research program is estuarine-related.[46] The National Science Foundation conducts wetlands research through four different programs, one of which, the Ecosystem Studies Program, is responsible for much of the funding to develop an integrated analysis of the Okefenokee Swamp in south Georgia.

All these agencies have mechanisms for establishing their individual wetland research priorities. They are also involved jointly in wetland symposia and several research projects. There is, however, no formal mechanism to provide for *interagency* coordination of wetland research.[47]

Summary of Federal Wetland Programs

Programs and policies of the federal government cut both ways with regard to the nation's wetland resources. The policy directives of President Carter were landmark acknowledgements by the executive branch of the importance of wetlands and the impact of federal activities on wetland environments. These policies, however, are incapable of providing concrete mechanisms by which agricultural and urban development can be managed in accordance with maintaining viable wetland resources. The CWA is the only such direct federal influence over wetland conversion pressures, but its mandate is vague and enforcement is weak in many respects. Furthermore, financial and technical assistance is provided to projects having contradictory objectives. Thus, with support of federal research funding and mapping capabilities, state and local governments may have to assert their interests by implementing wetland protection mechanisms based on legitimate concerns for the public health, safety, and welfare.

STATE WETLAND PROGRAMS

Federal wetland programs' insufficiencies have prompted several state and local governments to intervene to ensure proper management of wetlands. State interests in wetland programs are further prompted by water quality and supply concerns, now within the domain of most states such as Georgia that have assumed CWA permitting responsibilities, and by interjurisdictional effects caused by a lack of local participation. State governments may also be in a better position than local governments to manage wetlands from the standpoint of having the expertise and finances to identify, evaluate, and manage impacts upon wetland resources.

Federal wetland programs and their shortcomings suggest possibilities for improving wetlands management through alternative strategies on state and local levels. The wetland management alternatives available to state and local governments include direct and indirect state regulatory measures and alternatives to regulatory controls such as public land management programs for wildlife and other purposes, wetland acquisition programs, and tax incentives.

Direct State Regulatory Measures

Many states have now adopted some form of regulatory control over coastal and/or inland wetland development. Almost all 30 coastal states (including those bordering the Great Lakes) have programs that directly or indirectly regulate the use of their coastal wetlands. At least 13 states, including Georgia, accomplish this through direct coastal wetland regulation statutes, requiring permits for designated regulated activities.[48] In Georgia "any alteration of marshlands" will require a permit from the Department of Natural Resources. These programs, in combination with the federal program to enforce section 404 of the Clean Water Act, provide reasonably effective protection for coastal wetlands.

Inland freshwater wetlands have not received consistent legislative recognition from all states. Eight states manage inland wetlands by statutes enacted explicitly for that purpose.[49] These statutes provide for direct state permitting authority with performance standards enforced by state authorities or by local governing authorities with state intervention only upon local inaction. Besides specific state inland wetlands laws, a number of states have adapted existing laws to include protection of freshwater wetlands.

Regulatory Justification

Regardless of enforcement authority, certain justifications underlie all wetland management initiatives. Protection of health and public safety is the overriding concern justifying state or local legislative action and arises from protective wetland functions such as flood control and water quality maintenance. Government obligations to ensure consistency between wetland activities and broader planning or regulatory efforts, to prevent nuisances from incompatible land uses, and to prevent extraordinary costs for municipal services such as roads, water supply, and sewage provide further support for state and local government concern with wetland development.

Approaches to Wetland Regulation

The many wetland functions upon which society depends and the presence or absence of such values among particular wetland types dictate a flexible regulatory approach. Some wetlands do not provide the overall values discussed in Chapter 2 and, as a result, their conversion to other uses may be appropriate. In other situations, the complete prohibition of uses is necessary to protect wetland functions. In these circumstances, purchase of the wetland may be the most acceptable protection mechanism, although, in some cases, regulatory prohibition of uses is possible. Generally, however, few wetland regulatory programs prohibit all public and private wetland activities. Rather, performance standards applied through a permitting process are principally relied upon to lessen impacts of particular concern. Regulatory agencies are given broad discretion in evaluating wetland development proposals, yet standards must be applied in a manner so as to provide some degree of certainty to wetland property owners. Both certainty and flexibility are achieved by the application of minimum performance standards with regard to certain statutorily created presumptions and a final weighing and balancing of competing concerns.[50]

Performance standards. A widely adopted alternative management strategy involves the use of less restrictive performance standards and development guidelines. Performance standards can be general in nature and apply to a wide range of wetland activities or may be implemented as specific standards applicable to particular uses. Table 11 provides examples of performance standards applicable within a permitting procedure.

Wetland impacts relative to the limits of a performance standard are determined by the application of quantitative and qualitative assessment criteria. Quantitative assessment criteria apply to impose limits on development density (lot size) and the percentage of impermeable surface in addition to maintaining water quality standards and flood protection elevations. Unquantified criteria include wildlife protection, aesthetic values, and other functions. The more specific the standard to which such criteria apply the less flexibility there is for administrative implementation.

Performance standards help to reduce wetland management to a concise and intelligible set of principles to which many factual circumstances are applicable. Such factual applicability individualizes permit considerations relative to the applicant's particular proposal and the effect on the specific values retained by the wetland in question. Other advantages to the use of performance standards are allowing a number of wetland-use options, engendering less political opposition, and being less vulnerable to constitutional challenges.

Performance standards, however, require a considerable level of expertise in administration and enforcement and may lead to failures to account for cumulative wetland impacts and inconsistencies in implementation. Qualitative performance standards create uncertainty regarding the permissible uses of wetlands.

Presumptions. Presumptions may be established in all or particular stages of the permit process requiring the applicant to show that his activities will not affect the wetland contrary to legislative standards or administratively promulgated performance standards. For example, Georgia's Marshland Protection Act requires the petitioner to affirmatively show that his actions "will not be contrary to the public interest."[51] Thus, marsh alterations are presumed contrary to the public interest until proven otherwise by the applicant. Other possibilities include requiring the permit applicant to show (1) alternative

Table 11: *Performance Standards for Protecting Wetland Functions*

General Standard	Common Activities and Processes Requiring Control	Impact of Uncontrolled Uses	Application of Standard
Prevent filling of wetland by sand, gravel, solid wastes, structures, etc.	1. Land fill operations. 2. Dredge and spoil disposal. 3. Construction of roads, dikes, dams, reservoirs. 4. Activities on adjacent land or in the watershed causing sedimentation such as agriculture operations, timber cutting, road building, urban runoff, mining operations, channelization.	1. Destruction of flood storage and flood conveyance capacity. 2. Accelerated runoff. 3. Destruction of wildlife and vegetative values. 4. Reduced ground water infiltration. 5. Destruction of scenic, recreation education, pollution control functions.	1. Prohibit or tightly control filling in all or selected types of wetland areas. 2. Prohibit activities which require fills such as dwellings, factories, and roads. 3. Establish wetland buffer zones or setbacks for fills and structures to reduce sedimentation from upland sources. 4. Regulate grading, topsoil removal, and vegetation removal in upland areas.
Protect wetland water supply (quantity)	1. Construction of upstream reservoirs. 2. Agricultural and other types of drainage. 3. Channelization of streams. 4. Pumping of streams, lakes, ground water supplies. 5. Establishment of dikes, levees, sea walls, blocking exchange of tidal flows, flood waters. 6. Mosquito control projects.	1. Destruction or deterioration of wetland vegetation. 2. Reduced aquifer recharge. 3. Disturbance or destruction of wildlife species that depend upon wetlands for breeding, feeding, and nutrients. 4. Increased salinity (in some instances) resulting in damage to wildlife, vegetation, recreation opportunities.	1. Regulate the construction of dams, drainage projects, stream channelization, water extractions. 2. Manage reservoirs and floodgates to maintain wetland supply.
Protect wetland soils	1. Dredging, channelizations. 2. Topsoil removal. 3. Construction of reservoirs. 4. Mining.	1. Disturbance or destruction of vegetation and wildlife habitat. 2. Increased water turbidity. 3. Decreased recreation, education, wildlife values.	1. Regulate dredging, lagooning, mining, wetland soil removal.
Maintain free circulation of wetland waters	1. Dikes, dams, levees, sea walls, roads. 2. Irrigation projects. 3. Fills, grading, buildings.	1. Deprive wetland plants and animals of nutrients from flood flows and other sources. 2. Prevent the feeding and breeding of aquatic species in wetland areas. 3. Build-up of salinity (in some instances).	1. Require that bridges and roads be constructed with minimum impediment to natural drainage. 2. Design floodgates and sea walls to maintain tidal action. 3. Regulate construction of dikes, levees. 4. Require wetland structures to be elevated on pilings.
Protect wetland vegetation from cutting, grading, etc.	1. Forestry (in some instances). 2. Cranberry cultivation. 3. Agriculture. 4. Off-the-road vehicles. 5. Filling, grading. 6. Soil removal.	1. Damage to wildlife habitat. 2. Reduced pollution filtering capability. 3. Increased water velocities, erosion. 4. Destruction of scenic values.	1. Control filling, grading, soil removal, pollution sources, and other activities which destroy the wetland substrate or the water quantity required for specific vegetation.

From John A. Kusler, *Our National Wetland Heritage: A Protection Guidebook,* Environmental Law Institute, 1983.

compensatory storage (such as upland reservoir or excavations) for any loss of flood storage occasioned by development; (2) necessity of or an overriding public interest in the development; and (3) compatibility of use with wetland type.

Weighing and balancing. Weighing and balancing of factors such as environmental and economic benefits and costs may be required of the permitting agency. Administrative agencies may also be required to consider the permit's consistency with broader regulatory goals, local land use and other plans, and public preferences. Weighing and balancing requirements generally serve to assure that the administrative agency has taken into account the specific considerations mandated by the legislature.

Specific Inland Wetland Legislation

As noted above, nine states now have laws directly addressing the inland freshwater wetlands within their respective borders: Connecticut, Florida, Maine, Massachusetts, Michigan, Minnesota, New Hampshire, New York, and Rhode Island. Although similar in their objectives, mechanisms for the implementation of each state's law differ considerably. These statutes either authorize the state regulatory agency to regulate wetlands directly or to adopt minimum standards for regulation by local governments. The latter approach authorizes direct state involvement only where the local authorities fail to adopt and enforce minimum standards.

Direct state-level implementation. Two states maintaining direct authority to implement their inland freshwater wetland legislation are New Hampshire and Rhode Island. New Hampshire's lead agency, the Wetlands Board, is authorized to promulgate rules and to issue permits for construction and other activities in coastal and inland wetland areas.[52] The rules differentiate between major and minimum impact projects in addition to varying the performance criteria for different types of wetlands. Violations of the New Hampshire law are misdemeanors and failure to obey a lawful order of the Wetlands Board may result in a fine not to exceed $5,000, which may be used for restoration costs, research, and investigations relative to wetlands.

Rhode Island's Fresh Water Wetlands Act of 1971[53] is administered by the Department of Environmental Management which promulgates rules and issues permits for wetland alterations. The department's jurisdiction extends to buffer areas around wetlands and along rivers and floodplains. Violators of the act are issued notice and given an opportunity for a hearing and are ultimately subject to repay state-initiated restoration costs plus a fine not to exceed $1,000. Rhode Island is recognized as having a highly effective wetlands law and is being considered by EPA for authorization to administer Section 404 permitting responsibilities under the CWA.

State-authorized local implementation. Most state inland freshwater wetland legislation has provided for local authority to implement standards established on the state level. In the event of local inaction, a state environmental agency is generally designated to administer and enforce the law for that locality. States that have enacted this type of wetland legislation include Connecticut, Florida, Maine, Massachusetts, Michigan, Minnesota, and New York.

Connecticut's Inland Wetlands and Water Courses Act[54] was enacted in 1972 and authorizes municipal inland wetland agencies to issue permits for construction and other activities significantly impacting wetland areas. The state Department of Environmental Protection directly manages wetlands in towns without wetland agencies and wetland alterations proposed by state agencies. Connecticut is unique in basing its wetlands definition entirely on soil types. Where local units fail to adopt rules conforming to state standards or fail to enforce those rules, that authority reverts back to the department. Violators may be ordered to cease activities or to remedy the conditions; willful violations may result in a fine not to exceed $1,000. These funds may be used to restore the affected wetland or watercourse.

Florida has recently passed wetlands legislation providing for local government participation in a permitting program. The Warren S. Henderson Wetlands Protection Act of 1984[55] established state-level permitting authority over dredging or filling "in, on, or over" surface waters of the state. Waters of the state are defined on the basis of soil and vegetative factors and are coextensive with wetlands jurisdiction except that the new legislation extends that jurisdiction to the ordinary or mean high-water line of such waters. Permit considerations include not only the impact of the project under review but also the cumulative impacts of prior and future projects within the area. Under the Florida program, local governments may administer and enforce the wetlands program but the state Department of Environmental Regulation retains exclusive permitting authority, although it may delegate such power if "necessary or desirable." Local governments are, nevertheless, given notice of permit applications and the opportunity to file objections, request a hearing, or participate as a party to any legal proceedings concerning the application for a permit. Violators of the act are subject to civil penalties in the form of compensation for environmental damage and penalties of $10,000 per day and to criminal penalties in the form of first degree misdemeanor, punishable by a fine of not less than $2,500 or more than $25,000 and/or one year in jail.

Maine manages the development of inland freshwater wetlands through three separate legislative enactments. Permits are required under the Stream Alteration Act[56] to dredge, fill, or erect a permanent structure in public waterways including nonpermanent or intermittent waterways such as wetlands. Wetland activities are further controlled under the Great Ponds Act.[57] This Act provides for consultation with local governments in the issuance of permits for construction activities within the normal high-water line of water bodies having a surface area of over 10 acres. Recent legislation in Maine provides the Department of Environmental Protection with the authority to regulate similar development activities in freshwater wetlands falling outside the definitional framework of the Stream Alteration Act and the Great Ponds Act.[58] Vegetative and soil characteristics are used to define regulated wetlands, the boundaries of which are delineated on official state maps. Municipalities are given the opportunity to administer and enforce the legislation in accordance with state-approved procedures and standards.

Massachusetts' Wetland Protection Act[59] was the nation's first law to regulate the alteration of inland freshwater wetlands. The state Department of Environmental Quality Engineering (DEQE) promulgates rules establishing standards which are administered by local conservation commissions. DEQE reviews orders and permits issued by the commissions and serves as the appeal agency in disputes over action or inaction of the conservation commission. Violators of this law incur a fine not to exceed $1,000 or imprisonment for not more than six months, or both.

Massachusetts overlaps this permitting program with blanket restrictions on encroachments for wetlands mapped and identified by the state Department of Environmental Management.[60] Under the Inland Wetlands Act, orders of restriction are issued for designated wetlands including buffer areas surrounding or adjacent to those wetlands. Orders of restriction are subject to amendment for which public hearings must be held.

After 12 consecutive years of unsuccessful efforts to pass wetlands legislation, Michigan's Wetland Protection Act[61] was passed and became effective in late 1980. The act requires a permit for development activities in wetland areas. Michigan's Department of Natural Resources (DNR) promulgates standards to be administered by municipalities choosing to enact implementing ordinances. Such municipalities may provide for more stringent standards than those promulgated by the state agency and are authorized to issue permits subject to DNR review. Municipalities without wetland ordinances are given the opportunity to review and make recommendations on permit applications. Violators are subject to court-ordered restoration in addition to a fine not to exceed $2,500. Willful violations are also misdemeanors but are subject to a fine of not less than $2,500 nor more than $25,000 or imprisonment for not more than a year, or both. A second violation is considered a felony punishable by a fine not to exceed $50,000 per day of violation or by imprisonment for not more than two years, or both.

Minnesota also provides for authorization for local governments to implement and enforce the state's Public Waters and Wetlands Permit Program.[62] The Permit Program authorizes the state Department of Natural Resources to inventory and regulate, by a permitting procedure, various activities below the ordinary high-water mark in Minnesota's wetlands. Regulated wetlands include and are limited to Circular 39 types 3, 4, and 5 (see Chapter 3) which are 10 or more acres in size for unincorporated areas, or 2.5 or more acres in size for incorporated areas. Local units of government may require development activities to acquire a permit and may impose stricter standards of performance for permitted activities. Violations of the Minnesota legislation constitute misdemeanors punishable by a fine of up to $500 and/or 90 days in jail.

New York's Freshwater Wetland Act[63] was enacted in 1975, but implementing rules and regulations were not promulgated by the Department of Environmental Conservation (DEC) until June of 1980. Permits are required for activities in freshwater wetlands or their adjacent areas; activities deemed to have only slight environmental impacts may proceed with "letters of permission" from the issuing authority. Upon completion and filing of freshwater wetland maps, a municipal or county government may adopt implementing ordinances and assume jurisdiction of the program. Counties may assume jurisdiction in the absence of municipal action; DEC takes over the program in lieu of county adoption or in the case of unique wetland areas. Wetlands of less than 12.4 acres (5 hectares) are not portrayed on official state maps but are reserved for local regulatory jurisdiction. Violations may be punished by requirements to restore the wetland area and/or a civil fine not to exceed $3,000. Criminal sanctions provide for a $1,000 fine for a first offense or a $2,000 fine for a second offense and/or a prison term not to exceed six months.

Indirect State Regulatory Measures

Most states do not have permitting programs directly concerned with the protection of freshwater wetlands. Freshwater wetlands may, however, receive indirect protection from regulatory efforts with other immediate objectives. Examples of indirect protection afforded freshwater wetlands include state influence on federal programs and other state programs that incidentally cover some development activities on some wetlands.

State influence on federal actions is, for most states, their most important means of controlling wetland use.[64] State certification of water projects through section 401 of the CWA and comments upon section 404 permit applications can be used as partial substitutes for state wetland programs. Federal projects are also required to assure consistency of their development with state coastal management programs.[65] Thus, South Carolina indirectly regulates freshwater wetlands in the coastal zone by protective policy statements in its Coastal Zone Act. All federal actions in the coastal zone, including 404 permitting, must be consistent with this policy.[66] Similarly, management plans and guidelines adopted by state agencies in California are used by the Corps in administering permitting programs in natural tidal and nontidal marshes and riparian areas.[67]

Other state regulatory programs can indirectly assist in managing freshwater wetlands. At least 30 states have adopted floodplain regulations or state standards for local regulations. Wetland impacts are not specifically considered and fill is generally permitted to the extent that flood elevations are not increased. Floodplain regulations can, however, protect riverine wetlands in flood hazard zones. Land use control in the floodplain has been implemented in hundreds of communities across the nation pursuant to the National Flood Insurance Program (NFIP). Other states provide indirect wetland protections through regional zoning laws for coastal areas, wild and scenic river laws, critical area legislation, and dam safety laws.

Alternatives to Regulatory Control

Valuable supplemental alternatives to regulatory control include several nonregulatory efforts such as programs for wildlife management, tax incentives, and wetland acquisition programs.

Wildlife Management Programs

Public land management programs for wildlife exist in all 50 states. Wetland related programs include wildlife protection areas, propagation and stocking of fish and waterfowl, rare and endangered species programs, and conservation education efforts. Many of these programs involve the acquisition and management of wetland areas. In Georgia, habitat acquisition funds are derived from the federal Endangered Species Act program and federal Pittman-Robertson funds and, under certain circumstances Dingell-Johnson funds. State funds for wetland acquisition were authorized during the 1985 session of the Georgia General Assembly with the passage of House Bill 96. This bill authorizes the Department of Natural Resources to develop an official waterfowl stamp for the state and to use the funds generated from this stamp to, among other things, acquire wetlands.

Tax Incentives

States may affect wetland and other land uses by way of estate taxes, gift taxes, income taxes, and real estate taxes. Because most state provisions are effective in much the same way as federal estate, gift, and income taxes, only state guidelines for property tax assessments will be discussed here. Preferential tax assessment policies for open space, agricultural, forestry, and other conservation lands are available in 44 states.[68] Preferential tax laws are designed to offset development pressures by reflecting use values rather than market values or "highest use values." Three approaches are utilized in providing these tax benefits.

"Pure" preferential assessment assesses eligible lands at present use value as opposed to market or highest and best use values. It is available to all qualified landowners and no penalties are suffered on withdrawal from the program.

Another approach, a deferred taxation system, taxes land at its present use value, but landowners of eligible land who convert their land to noneligible uses must pay some or all of the taxes that would have otherwise accrued during the years of preferential assessment.

A third system of tax assessment involves restrictive agreements entered into by qualifying landowners to restrict the development of the area for a number of years. Land under the agreement is assessed either at zero or at the present use value but also requires payment of deferred taxes upon conversion to non-eligible uses. This approach has been used in Georgia for the preferential assessment of agricultural land.[69]

In 1981, the Oregon legislature enacted two mechanisms to encourage the maintenance or rehabilitation of privately owned wetlands.[70] First, it provides an ad valorem property tax exemption for riparian lands that are protected and, second, it grants a 25 percent personal or corporate income tax credit for costs incurred in fish habitat improvement projects.[71] Withdrawal of land from the program requires payment of up to five times the amount of taxes due on the exempted property during the most recent tax year.[72] To minimize the fiscal loss of the ad valorem tax shift, three restrictions were incorporated into the law: (1) lands eligible must be designated forest or farmlands outside of identified urban growth boundaries, (2) lands exempted can be no more than 100 feet from the line of non-aquatic vegetation, and (3) no more than 100 miles of streambank can be exempted each year in any one county. Total dollar limits were also placed on taxpayers benefiting from the exemptions.

Preferential tax assessment systems must provide adequate incentive to the landowner for maintaining the undeveloped wetlands and yet prevent the use of the system as a tax dodge. Otherwise, lands will remain undeveloped only until development pressures and market values reach profitability levels. The disincentive for conversion provided by the deferred taxation and restrictive agreement approaches is preferable in this regard.

Wetland Acquisition

Wetland acquisition by fee or easement interest is perhaps the most protective measure available to state and local governments. Acquisition may be accomplished by gift, devise, or purchase. Systematic wetland purchase programs should involve careful preliminary inventories and assessments to maximize the benefits available from state and community funds. Acquisition in fee gives total public control over the wetland; easements may also permit public access. Public purchase of wetlands, however, can be extremely expensive. Local governments suffer further losses of revenue by removing the area from the tax rolls.

Summary of State Wetland Programs

State laws for managing freshwater wetlands have intervened to compensate for the legal and administrative insufficiencies of federal wetland programs. Several states have adopted legislation specifically addressing their freshwater wetlands. Many more states have only indirect control over their wetland resource by means of flood plain regulations and various ways of influencing federal regulatory programs. Public land management, tax incentives, and wetland acquisition programs are also important alternatives to states wishing to manage more effectively their important wetland environments.

LOCAL GOVERNMENT WETLAND PROGRAMS

At the local level, wetland protection is best integrated with broader community land use planning. Because of the traditional and still pervasive view of wetlands as a land rather than a water resource and because traditional and current land use planning objectives are within their domain, local governments have an interest to assert in wetland resource management programs. Most state wetland programs incorporate significant elements of local involvement. The freshwater wetland enabling statutes of Massachusetts, Connecticut, New York, and other states place primary responsibility for regulation on local levels of government.

Local governments are generally considered "creatures of the state" and can only exercise those powers delegated to them by the state legislature. Local regulation of wetland development activities is accomplished pursuant to state law in one of two ways. General authorizations from state constitutions or statutes are responsible for the local exercise of police power protections of public health and safety, under which several methods of control can be asserted. Specific state wetland statutes provide another avenue by which local governments are vested with control over permitting and other responsibilities.

Local Police Power Regulation

Wetland regulations issued pursuant to the local government's police authority can take the form of performance standards or complete prohibitions of certain uses. Performance standards are most common and are instituted by zoning, subdivision regulation, and building and sanitary codes.

Zoning

Wetland zoning regulations, adopted as part of a comprehensive zoning ordinance, are the most common type of local control mechanisms. Such regulations first designate, by mapping or by text description, those areas to which regulatory measures will be applied. Lists of prohibited uses are specified and those areas are typically made subject to general performance standards such as lot size requirements, structure limitations, and drainage standards. The planning board will evaluate proposed developments in terms of the resource values affected and the possible adverse consequences to neighboring properties. Because evaluations of development impact may be handicapped by limitations in budgets, data bases, and expertise, many local ordinances will require the developer to do some site assessment work. The success of many local wetland regulatory programs will often depend on outside assistance in mapping wetlands and assessing development impacts.

Floodplain zoning is also common, but is usually applicable only to mapped flood zones along major streams and rivers. These zones often extend to the limits of the 100-year floodplain, which by the standards of the National Flood Insurance Program (NFIP), qualifies the local government for federally subsidized flood insurance. Wetlands not associated with rivers or streams, however, would not benefit from the usual floodplain zoning ordinance. Where explicit regulatory objectives do not provide for wetland protection, minor floodplain zoning amendments could often strengthen wetland protection by extending floodplain controls over structures, fills, and dredging to isolated wetland areas.[73] Otherwise, a separate wetland zoning ordinance would provide the necessary overlap.

Subdivision Regulations

Subdivision regulations are adopted on a community-wide basis and may contain provisions effective in managing the development of local wetland resources. Builders are typically required to prepare detailed maps or ''plats'' and to obtain approval from a local planning board prior to division or sale. Factors considered include lot size and width, access roads, suitability of the land for development, drainage, flooding, and adequate public facilities. Subdivision regulations can also provide for the clustering of buildings in upland areas while maintaining overall density by leaving low-lying wetland or floodplain areas free from structural development.

Building and Sanitary Codes

Building and sanitary codes can be used to conform development to uses consistent with maintaining the natural functions and values associated with wetland areas. Building code requirements may provide that structures be elevated above flood hazard levels and that suitable foundation material be used to locate them. Sanitary codes can be most effective in controlling the development of rural wetlands where septic tanks and soil absorption systems should not be located in high ground water areas or near lakes and streams.

State Wetland Management Acts

Local regulation of development in wetland areas is authorized by state law in Connecticut, Florida, Maine, Massachusetts, Michigan, Minnesota, and New York. Wisconsin and Washington also require the local implementation of less protective wetland legislation.[74] In addition, many other local governments have adopted land use regulations under authorities of the Coastal Zone Management Act and the National Flood Insurance Program.[75]

Summary of Local Wetland Programs

Local governments manage their wetlands resource by having such authority delegated to them by the state. The traditional delegation of land use prerogatives to local governments is a major source of this authority as is the police power authority to provide for the public health, safety, and welfare. Implementation of these powers often takes the form of zoning ordinances, subdivision regulations, and building or sanitary codes. Other states, however, give local governments the specific authority to assume responsibility for managing wetlands under the authority of state wetland protection legislation.

As pointed out in the wetlands case law discussion in Chapter 4, federal, state, and local regulation can be found to unconstitutionally "take" a landowner's property without just compensation. This issue can be avoided in several ways. As with state laws and regulations, the local government should use performance standards rather than completely prohibiting all structural uses of wetland areas. Negotiations between the governmental body and the landowner regarding the size, design, and precise location of the development can preclude litigation and also educate citizens about the rational need for careful management of wetland environments. In addition, local governments can coordinate regulations with state tax policies to lessen the financial burden of restrictive wetland controls.

6 Wetland Management Alternatives for Georgia

Given the values associated with wetlands and the substantial rate of conversion of wetlands to other uses in Georgia, consideration should be given to evaluating more precisely the condition of wetlands in the state and determining if some form of wetland protection measures should be instituted. Investigations are needed to locate and evaluate wetland environments in Georgia, to analyze the potential for their conversion and degradation, and to explore in detail the alternatives available for managing the state's extensive wetlands resource wisely. Since many levels of government may be involved in wetland conversion or protection activities and because of the variety of wetlands and the types of pressures on them, exploring a wide range of alternatives is essential. Viable regulatory, administrative, financial, and educational alternatives are available to accomplish prudent wetland management objectives.

REGULATORY ALTERNATIVES

The police power duties of state and local governments require that wetland resources be managed with due regard for the public health, safety, and welfare (see Chapter 4). In this context, the relationship of wetlands to such environmental and socioeconomic values as water quality and flood control suggests that state and local governments should exercise these powers to provide for the orderly and limited development of wetland areas within their jurisdiction. Constitutional authority in Georgia rests with the General Assembly to provide by law for "[r]estriction upon land use in order to protect and preserve the natural resources, environment, and vital areas of this state" (Art. II, Sec. VI, Par. II). Otherwise, constitutional authorizations for land use controls are vested solely with local governmental entities.

Wetland regulatory approaches are generally designed to require an evaluation of a proposed use, in order to permit those uses which will not adversely alter the wetland resource and to deny uses which will have a significant adverse effect. In light of the particularity of different wetland environments, this will require identification of the values inherent in specific wetlands, the potential effect of a proposed activity upon those values, and the alternatives available to mitigate or prevent the adverse consequences of the proposed use. Federal, state, and local governments have instituted regulatory programs affecting wetlands, such as the Corps of Engineers 404 permit program, state wetland protection programs, and local land use ordinances.

Corps of Engineers 404 Program

As discussed in Chapter 4, the Corps' 404 permitting program is substantially deficient with regard to the protection given to the nation's wetland resources. Most importantly, the Corps needs an explicit wetlands jurisdictional directive from Congress and, with it, additional funding to effectively carry it out. Because it is currently in the business of regulating wetland activities, albeit to a limited degree, the Corps of Engineers is the federal agency in the best position to extend the jurisdictions of wetland regulations into those areas and activities that now create a significant vacuum in the 404 permitting program. Preliminarily, however, the Corps could act without congressional directive to administer more effectively and consistently the 404 program, set priorities for monitoring and enforcing its provisions, and promote public awareness of the agency's mission with respect to wetlands and the 404 program.

State Wetland Protection Laws

Following the release of the 1956 Fish and Wildlife Service report, national concern was increasingly focused upon the conversion of wetlands to other uses. It was not until the early 1960s, however, that attempts to protect wetlands were undertaken by states. As might be expected, the more populated northeastern states were among the first to adopt any form of wetland protection laws: Massachusetts (1963), Rhode Island (1965), and Connecticut (1969). These first laws addressed only coastal wetlands.

Georgia became the fourth state in the nation to enact a coastal wetlands act with the passage of the Marshlands Protection Act in 1970. Although a number of concerns were evident on the coast, the major impetus for the enactment of this law was a proposal to mine phosphates in the marshes in Chatham County. In a report to the governor, a University System of Georgia committee stressed the value of the salt marshes to Georgia and identified the marginal economic impact that phosphate mining would have on the state if the phosphate was not refined within Georgia.[1] As a result, the mining was prohibited under the state's water quality law and, to ensure protection of the salt marshes, the General Assembly passed the Marshlands Protection Act (MPA). Coastal wetland values have now been recognized in all coastal and Great Lakes states except Texas, Ohio, and Illinois by the adoption of some form of coastal wetland protection laws.

Thus, the state of Georgia has in place a program to stop the indiscriminate alteration of coastal marshlands. The effectiveness of this program is largely due to the strong enforcement efforts of the Coastal Division of DNR. In 1984, a legislative study committee reviewed the state's coastal management efforts and determined that, although some improvements might be made, the Marshlands Protection Act was working well and no amendments would be introduced. In the future, however, consideration may be given to expanding the wetlands protected under this law to include freshwater wetlands that interact with the brackish and salt marshes, which was not considered by the legislative study committee.

Since the coastal salt marshes have already been addressed by the state, this discussion focuses on alternatives to protect inland freshwater wetlands in Georgia. Freshwater wetlands have generally received less attention than coastal marshlands. This situation changed, however, when the U.S. Department of Agriculture's practice of draining wetlands for agricultural purposes was brought into question in the early 1970s. The implementation of these practices along portions of the Alcovy River in northeast Georgia became the focal point of a national controversy over wetland drainage. Based on Wharton's studies assessing the values of the Alcovy bottomland forest,[2] the proposed drainage of these riverine lands was abandoned. Unlike the controversy surrounding the coastal marshes, however, no law was subsequently enacted to protect freshwater wetlands in Georgia.

States have approached freshwater wetland protection in two ways: by enacting a specific freshwater wetlands protection statute and by adapting existing state laws to provide for protection of freshwater wetlands.

State Freshwater Wetland Laws

Currently, eight states have enacted freshwater wetland protection laws. The only southeastern state with such a law is Florida. Common characteristics of these laws include defining wetlands, mapping, the permitting of wetland alterations, and enforcement procedures and penalties for noncompliance. Some states enable local governments to implement these freshwater wetlands laws if they establish the capability to do so.

Defining wetlands. Defining wetlands is important in determining what wetlands will be included under the law. As may be expected, wetlands are defined differently by states. New York depends exclusively on vegetation for defining and delimiting wetlands. Other states use a combination of vegetation, hydrology, and soils. Professional assessments based on site investigations are generally required to determine the precise location of wetland boundaries.

States vary in the size required for wetlands to be considered under the law. These range from having no lower limit to having a minimum of 12.4 acres

(5 hectares) in New York. Although placing a minimum size on wetlands to be included under the law may be a practical mechanism to ensure consideration of major wetlands, the value of smaller wetlands may not be reflected by their size (for example, the ground water pollution potential of limesinks). From a resource management perspective, the total exclusion of smaller wetlands from a regulatory program is unjustified; from a constitutional perspective it may be discriminatory or unreasonable to regulate wetlands of different sizes possessing identical values (see Chapter 4).

Mapping wetlands. Mapping of wetlands is a basic component of any management strategy. Wetland mapping, however, can be a major undertaking requiring several years to identify and delimit wetlands in the state. Coastal wetlands, salt, brackish, and freshwater, have been mapped by the Department of Natural Resources and by the FWS National Wetlands Inventory. The FWS is in the process of producing maps of the coastal wetlands.[3] Landsat data is also available to state and local governments having the capability to tap into the computerized data base. In addition, many of the riverine wetlands have been mapped through the National Flood Insurance Program which requires identification of the 100-year flood zone. Although the floodplain identified may differ from the defined wetland limit and the quality of the mapping effort may be less than desired, these maps provide a base for the development of more detailed maps, if necessary. Also, some mapping of the location of Carolina bays and limesinks has been done in the state. Mapping of Georgia's wetlands could build on these previous efforts.

Mapping of wetlands is very important in that it determines which areas will come under the purview of the program. Most states have found it important that wetlands be accurately translated to map locations, some to the extent that in-house mapping of the entire state is undertaken. Such efforts are needless when slight modifications of existing maps may suffice to provide adequate notice to private landowners and to guide state or local officials in the actual on-site delimitation of the particular wetland. The actual boundary of the wetland is less important from a management standpoint if the law includes a buffer zone of a certain width (e.g., 100 feet) bordering the wetland. Buffer zone requirements would also help to lessen disputes over precise boundaries, in which relatively minor variations can involve significant economic consequences.

Permit evaluation. Evaluating permit applications will necessitate on-site inspections of the proposed activity. This will require trained personnel in regional offices of DNR or trained local employees if the program is to be implemented by local governments (as it is in some states).

Evaluation of wetlands and the impacts of proposed activities is a necessary but difficult task. Although wetland managers and scientists are generally supportive of the ''Adamus method'' being perfected by the Federal Highway Administration, no consensus is evident on the specifics of evaluating wetlands, such as which factors are to be included in the evaluation, or whether the use of a numerical rating system is appropriate in making final permit determinations.[4] Any objective evaluation of freshwater wetlands should concisely identify their major values. General criteria that should be considered include the following:

1. Environmental protection values: Major environmental protection values accrue from wetlands that protect or enhance the quality of state waters. Wetlands that perform waste assimilation functions near urban areas, wetlands that serve as filters for non-point source pollutants because of their location between sources of contaminated runoff and streams, and wetlands such as limesinks which if contaminated would likely result in the contamination of other water resources, all should be given high priority. Based on these considerations, riverine and limesink wetlands particularly require a close evaluation of their environmental protection values.

2. Socioeconomic values: The major socioeconomic factor to be considered is likely to be the flood control capability of the wetland resource. Flood control values will vary widely from wetland to wetland. Because of their proximity to flood waters, riverine wetlands will generally rate higher than other wetlands on the socioeconomic scale.

3. Fish and wildlife values: The value of a wetland to fish and wildlife is a function of the food and habitat it provides and its relationship to adjacent ecosystems. Thus, isolated wetlands may be extremely valuable to wildlife because they differ from surrounding ecosystems. So too, riverine wetlands provide continuous corridors for wildlife to move from one area to another. The importance of wetland environments to wildlife experiencing rapidly declining habitat is well established but because many wetland types are capable of providing these values, each wetland will require individual evaluation.

From these permit evaluation criteria it appears that riverine and limesink wetlands generally provide the greatest service to Georgians and are likely to rate higher on any objective evaluation of freshwater wetlands. Regardless of whether a state freshwater wetland law is adopted, any wetland management alternative taken will necessitate the implementation of an objective evaluation mechanism by which each wetland can be analyzed to determine its specific value to the local community and to the state.

Enforcement and compliance. Enforcement is essential to the success of any state program for managing wetland resources. Effective enforcement of wetland laws or ordinances requires manpower and, consequently, financial support. Volunteer members of conservation commissions in several northeastern states provide manpower at little or no cost to the state or local government so that governmental surveillance costs are significantly reduced. As with any law, local communities must understand the importance of their wetland resource and the need for wise management if the law is to be effectively implemented. Strong public education programs should precede legal enforcement.

Additionally, imposition of penalties will be required for violations of the law. Most laws or ordinances provide for a combination of fines and possible jail sentences for varying degrees of noncompliance. Many ordinances also require some level of restoration of the wetland environment.

Delegating the wetlands program to local governments. A number of states have included provisions in their freshwater wetland laws granting local governments the authority to implement the program. Effectiveness of this approach varies from state to state. In Massachusetts, town conservation commissions have enthusiastically assumed the responsibility of managing wetlands within their jurisdiction.[5] In New York, local governments have been less effective in assuming wetland management authority, due in part to the slow progress made in mapping wetlands by the state Department of Environmental Conservation.[6] Wisconsin depends on the regional staff of its Department of Natural Resources to implement the freshwater wetlands management program.[7]

Given the opportunity, those local governments in Georgia with experience in developing comprehensive land use plans and with well-designed, effective zoning ordinances are likely to seek authority to implement the wetlands management program. If the state provided both technical assistance and financial support for the program, more local governments would likely seek implementation authority.

Adaptation of Existing Laws to Protect Wetlands

A number of states have adapted existing laws to provide some protection for freshwater wetlands. In Vermont, this approach has not worked very well[8] while in Pennsylvania provisions in existing laws give wetlands greater protection than in some states with specific wetland protection laws.[9]

Existing laws in Georgia relating directly or indirectly to wetlands include the Water Quality Control Act, the Ground Water Use Act, the Safe Drinking Water Act, the Erosion and Sedimentation Control Act, and the Metropolitan Rivers Protection Act. The process by which decisions are made pursuant to these laws can have a significant impact on wetlands. By considering potential impacts during the implementation process, unnecessary adverse effects might be avoided.

Water Quality Control Act. The Water Quality Control Act (WQCA) is the state law designed to protect the quality of surface waters in Georgia. Decisions made under this law affect the amount and types of discharges into the "waters of the state," including non-point sources of contamination. Wetlands are clearly within the statutory definition of "waters of the state" and are thus subject to protection from sources of pollution.

The WQCA also provides measures to assure the maintenance of sufficient quantities of surface water. Withdrawals in excess of 100,000 gallons of water per day must be permitted under the WQCA. Wetlands subjected to drainage threats from such upstream surface water withdrawals could be managed with permit limitations under this provision of the act. The WQCA could, therefore, be used to manage wetlands known to perform vital public functions.

Ground Water Use Act. The Georgia Ground Water Use Act is peculiarly adapted to maintain conservative quantities of Georgia's ground water resources. Ground water withdrawals may lower water levels where the wetland environment is hydrologically connnected to the ground water resource. Permit requirements for ground water withdrawals in excess of 100,000 gallons of water per day could be used to condition the permits of all water users (agriculture is exempted from these requirements) upon maintaining capacities and characteristics of the aquifer where wetlands contribute directly to them.

Safe Drinking Water Act. Contamination of public water systems is controlled and prohibited under the Safe Drinking Water Act. One practice allegedly used to illegally drain wetlands in Georgia is to simply drill a well in a wetland allowing the water to drain into the underlying aquifer. Because this water may be below the state's drinking water standards and lead to contamination of the aquifer, this practice can be considered an illegal injection of contaminants into a public water system.

Erosion and Sedimentation Act. The purpose of the Erosion and Sedimentation Act is to reduce soil erosion from various land disturbing activities and subsequent sedimentation into state waters. Insofar as the act "minimizes" the stripping of vegetation and cut and fill operations, and encourages the maintenance of natural vegetation buffers, wetlands are afforded some measure of protection. Maintenance of vegetative buffers along waterways is an effective mechanism to intercept eroded sediments and coincides with the natural erosion control and sediment trapping functions performed by riverine wetland systems.

Metropolitan Rivers Protection Act. The Metropolitan Rivers Protection Act regulates land disturbing activities in the floodplain of the Chattahoochee River for that part of the river flowing through the Atlanta metropolitan area. The act allows development in accordance with a comprehensive land and water use plan adopted by the Atlanta Regional Commission which, upon application, may recommend issuance of a certificate allowing the proposed use. A proposal to develop within 2,000 feet of the watercourse, or within the floodplain (whichever is greater), must establish that it is not harmful to the water and land resources of the stream corridor, will not significantly impede the natural flow of flood waters, and will not result in significant erosion. Buffer areas as determined by local governing authorities and ordinances implementing the Soil Erosion and Sedimentation Act are effective in the drainage basins of tributaries outside the stream corridor. Maintenance of water retention acreage for flood control purposes and buffer areas for erosion control may allow the preservation of riverine wetlands and their associated flood and erosion control values. Adaptation of this approach to other rivers in the state would provide some protection not only for riverine wetlands but also for the flood-prone property owners, municipal water supply systems, and the associated taxpayers who benefit from their preservation.

All of these laws relate directly or indirectly to freshwater wetlands in Georgia. Decisions pursuant to these regulatory laws can be made in light of their effect on wetlands as well as other considerations. By so doing, adverse impacts on freshwater wetlands may be minimized.

Local Land Use Ordinances

The Georgia Constitution (Art. IX, Sec. II, Par. IV) provides that "[t]he governing authority of each county and of each municipality may adopt plans and may exercise the power of zoning." The authority to plan and zone can be a significant tool for local governments to prevent the unnecessary conversion of freshwater wetlands through the assertion of their police power obligations. Zoning ordinances can be used to direct development away from wetland areas that protect local property owners from flood damage or from wetlands serving to enhance the quality of municipal water supplies. Zoning ordinances are often the mechanism by which 445 local governments in Georgia restrict floodplain development so as to qualify for flood insurance under the National Flood Insurance Program (NFIP). Comprehensive land use plans can be used to identify wetlands and flood prone areas and enable their protection within an overall framework of community land use.

Other police power controls over land use such as building permits and subdivision regulations can be used to mitigate impacts on freshwater wetlands. Both are acceptable regulatory options for complying with NFIP standards.

Coastal communities in Georgia are in the fortunate position of having their wetland resources at least partially mapped by the Department of Natural Resources and the FWS (see Chapter 3). An overlay of these wetland maps with the territory encompassed by the county or municipality would let the local government investigate and to some degree analyze their wetland resources. Landsat mapping is also available through relatively inexpensive personal computers for states investing in a centralized Landsat data base. This Landsat data base has been used by the Department of Community Affairs to aid Area Planning and Development Commissions and local governments in their planning efforts and has considerable potential for land use planning by local governments with a minimum of financial investment.

Local ordinances controlling land use will require that local government officials know where wetlands are located within their community and appreciate the wetland values. To aid local governments, the state could take an affirmative role in providing financial incentives and technical assistance for addressing wetland concerns.

ADMINISTRATIVE WETLAND PROTECTION MEASURES

As previously discussed, a number of state laws relate directly or indirectly to wetlands. Thus, the somewhat incidental activities of many state agencies administering their responsibilities may directly or indirectly affect wetlands. As a result, the daily operation of state business can have a significant influence on freshwater wetlands. Simply requiring state administrators to take into consideration the effects of their actions on freshwater wetlands could help prevent the degradation and conversion of some wetlands. Similar to President Carter's executive orders regarding wetlands and flood management, an executive order from the governor could direct state agencies to consider the impact of their activities on freshwater wetlands and to take such actions as needed to avoid causing the unnecessary degradation of these wetlands or their conversion to other uses. Such a policy statement could also serve to channel 404 permitting actions by the Corps of Engineers to coincide with that policy. A precedent for this was established when Governor Busbee issued an executive order requiring state agencies to consider their impacts on prime farmland and to take actions so as not to unnecessarily cause the conversion of these lands to nonagricultural uses.[10]

Regardless of its impact upon the administrative process, a substantive wetlands policy statement from the state's chief executive would alert Georgia's public officials and others to the environmental and economic importance of wetland resources. Some form of interagency mechanism to coordinate these actions and to resolve disputes would be necessary.

FINANCIAL ALTERNATIVES

Wetlands law is land use law (see Chapter 4) and consequently government is in the position of balancing the public good obtained from regulating wetlands against the rights of private landowners to use their property as they wish. Since in some cases restrictions placed on the use of wetlands may be considered a ''taking,'' mechanisms have been developed to compensate landowners for excessive restrictions on the use of their land. Financial alternatives for protecting wetlands include the outright purchase of the wetland and financial incentives and disincentives encouraging wetland protection.

Ownership of Wetlands

Public ownership provides the greatest protection for wetlands. This is the approach used in protecting the coastal marshes. These marshes have been found to be owned by the people of Georgia and are managed by the Coastal Division of the Georgia Department of Natural Resources under legal authority provided by the 1970 Marshlands Protection Act. Under this law, anyone desiring to undertake a project which would result in an alteration of the marshes is required to obtain a permit from the Department of Natural Resources. This process allows DNR to evaluate the potential impacts from the proposed development and determine if a permit should be issued with or without modifications or whether the permit must be denied.

Ownership of wetlands is also the major protective mechanism for the Okefenokee Swamp system. Over 93 percent of this wetland is owned and managed by the Fish and Wildlife Service as a National Wildlife Refuge. The Georgia Department of Natural Resources owns a portion of the swamp and manages it as a state park. In both cases, use restrictions are employed and the swamp is protected from conversion to other uses.

Most riverine and inland wetlands in the state are not in public ownership and, therefore, these wetlands are subject to market forces that generally do not factor the public interest into their decision-making processes. Some of these wetlands are purchased by the Department of Natural Resources with funds allocated for fish and wildlife management areas, from the waterfowl stamp program, and soon from the yet to be implemented Non-Game Income Tax Check-off system. Wetland environments could be given priority consideration under Georgia's already existing programs for public land purchases.

Financial Incentives and Disincentives

Regulatory approaches are generally utilized to prevent urban development in wetlands, while nonregulatory approaches are used to address conversion of wetlands for agricultural and forestry production. This is an important consideration in Georgia where 80 to 90 percent of wetland conversions probably result from agricultural and forestry activities.

The incentive to convert wetlands for row crop production comes primarily from the demand for greater production. This has been spurred on by governmental policies encouraging "fence row to fence row production." Governmental programs related to the expansion of export markets, institution of price supports and commodity reserves, and credit policies which encourage farmers to incur debts that require greater production to repay have led to the conversion and degradation of wetlands.

One approach to addressing this concern was recently considered by Congress. Legislation sponsored by Congressman Lindsay Thomas (Democrat, Ga.), known as the "swampbuster" provision of the 1985 omnibus farm bill, removed federal incentives for agricultural production from wetlands. Debate centered on the extent to which federal support would be lost, and on which lands were to be defined as wetlands. This approach when implemented could significantly aid in protecting the nation's wetland resources.

Conversion of wetlands for forestry production relates primarily to the drainage of hardwood bottoms and replanting them to pine stands. By draining the bottomland, the influx of nutrients which makes these wetlands productive is eliminated, resulting in a decline in the productive capability of the land. Although this seems self-defeating, the basic reason for converting these wetlands relates to the marketability of the products. In Georgia, there are markets for softwoods but few for hardwoods. Bozeman[11] hypothesized that the development of hardwood markets in Georgia would do more for protecting riverine wetlands from conversion to pine plantations than probably any other approach. Development of hardwood markets is a priority concern of the Georgia Forestry Commission.[12]

Besides removing incentives for farmers and foresters to convert wetlands to other uses, alternatives can be considered to provide incentives for them to maintain wetlands in their natural state. The approach implemented in Oregon to provide ad valorem tax incentives to riverine wetland owners who agree not to convert their wetlands to other uses might be usable in Georgia. This approach is already used for farmland in the state which is assessed at 30 percent of true market value rather than 40 percent if the landowner agrees not to convert the agricultural land to nonfarm uses. Compensating the landowner for protecting wetlands could significantly decrease the conversion of wetlands to agricultural and softwood forest uses.

EDUCATIONAL ALTERNATIVES

One of the major reasons for the degradation of wetlands and their conversion to other uses is a lack of understanding of the values of wetlands and the problems that their conversion might cause. Because of this, educational efforts can accomplish a great deal. For this to work, however, a state agency such as the Department of Natural Resources would have to receive financial support to institute an educational program itself or in cooperation with other organizations interested in wetland preservation.

7 Conclusions

Analyzing the wetland situation in Georgia makes it possible to determine (1) the nature and extent of wetlands in the state; (2) the values associated with these wetlands; (3) the forces acting upon these wetlands to cause their degradation or conversion; (4) the rate and extent of wetland conversion to other uses; and (5) the legal, administrative, and economic alternatives to address wetland problems in Georgia.

Analysis of data generated by the Georgia Department of Natural Resources, the U.S. Fish and Wildlife Service, and the U.S. Soil Conservation Service shows that Georgia is geographically dimorphic with respect to wetlands: the northern portion of the state has few wetlands while the southern portion has extensive wetlands. Wetlands in north Georgia consist primarily of riverine wetlands. Besides coastal salt marshes, south Georgia has riverine wetlands and inland wetlands consisting of cypress and gum ponds, Carolina bays, and limesinks. One of the most extensive freshwater systems in the country, the Okefenokee Swamp, is located in the southeastern part of the state. Other major wetlands in Georgia were also identified. Overall, Georgia ranks fourth among the conterminous states in total wetland acreage, with some 5.3 million acres. The importance of these wetlands is found in their environmental, fish and wildlife, and socioeconomic values.

Degradation forces acting upon wetlands are primarily point and non-point pollution sources which contaminate the wetland system. Conversion of wetlands to other uses results primarily from agricultural and forestry practices, urban development, hydroelectric reservoir construction, and dredging for navigation purposes.

Between the mid-1950s and the mid-1970s, the FWS estimates that 146,597 acres of Georgia wetlands, or 2.7 percent of the mid-1950s total, were converted to other uses. This amounts to an annual conversion rate of 7,300 acres. Considering the expansion of agricultural irrigation, bottomland drainage for pine production, construction of hydroelectric projects, expanded navigational dredging activities, and increased urban development, it is likely that the rate of wetland conversion to other uses has increased substantially during the decade since the mid-1970s.

The analysis of wetlands case law and statutory law indicates the state has the authority to protect wetlands from degradation and conversion to other uses. Regulatory land use control approaches are usually employed to prevent the conversion of wetlands to urban uses, based on the flood hazards associated with urban development in wetlands. Nonregulatory incentive programs are more frequently used to decrease the rate of wetland conversion to agricultural and pine production. The state has exercised its authority to protect saltwater wetlands with the passage of the 1970 Marshlands Protection Act but no such protection has been afforded freshwater wetlands in Georgia.

From this study, it is apparent that the wetlands of Georgia, particularly freshwater wetlands, have not been adequately quantified, mapped, or analyzed in regard to the environmental, fish and wildlife, and socioeconomic values they provide to the state. Attempts to quantify the values of wetlands, however, indicate that freshwater wetlands provide the same range of values as salt marshes that have been afforded protection, $10,000-30,000 per acre per year in goods and services. Since a significant amount of wetland conversion is under way and all indications are that conversion pressures will increase in the future, it is advisable for the state to undertake a more detailed analysis of its wetland resources. Such a project could more accurately identify and map valuable wetlands and develop a management program providing adequate protection to those wetlands of significant value to the state.

Notes

Chapter 2

1. Office of Technology Assessment, *Wetlands: Their Use and Regulation*, 28.
2. Ralph W. Tiner, Jr., *Wetlands of the United States: Current Status and Recent Trends*, 3.
3. M.T. Brown, and E.M. Starnes, *A Wetland Study of Seminole County*, 8.
4. L.M. Cowardin, V. Carter, F.C. Golet, and E.T. LaRoe, *Classification of Wetlands and Deepwater Habitats of the United States.*
5. Samuel P. Shaw and C. Gordon Fredine, *Wetlands of the United States: Their Extent and Their Value to Waterfowl and other Wildlife.*
6. Henry Sather, United States Department of the Interior, Fish and Wildlife Service, presentation at National Wetland Assessment Symposium, June 19, 1985.
7. K.G. Boto and William H. Patrick, Jr., "Role of Wetlands in the Removal of Suspended Sediments," in: *Wetland Functions and Values: The State of Our Understanding*, Proceedings of the National Symposium on Wetlands, Greeson et al., eds. (American Water Resources Association, 1979).
8. R.R. Grant, Jr. and R. Patrick, "Tinicum Marsh as a Water Purifier," *Two Studies of Tinicum Marsh, Delaware and Philadelphia Counties, Pennsylvania*, J. McCormick et al., eds. (The Conservation Foundation, 1970).
9. Mark T. Brown, University of Florida, presentation at National Wetland Assessment Symposium, June 19, 1985.
10. C.H. Wharton, *The Southern River Swamp—A Multiple Use Environment*, Bureau of Business and Economic Research, School of Business Administration, Georgia State University, Atlanta, Georgia, 1970.
11. John M. Hefner and James D. Brown, "Wetland Trends in the Southeastern United States."
12. Wharton, *Natural Environments of Georgia.*
13. Ibid.
14. Ibid.
15. Ibid.
16. Office of Technology Assessment, *Wetlands*, 58.
17. Ibid.
18. Jon A. Kusler. *Our National Wetland Heritage: A Protection Guidebook* (Environmental Law Insititute, 1983), 57.
19. Elon S. Verry and Don H. Boelter, "Peatland Hydrology," in *Wetland Functions and Values.*
20. Richard Novitzki, U.S. Geological Survey, presentation at National Wetland Assessment Symposium, June 19, 1985.
21. Office of Technology Assessment, *Wetlands*, 48.
22. Robert L. Johnson, "Timber Harvests From Wetlands," in *Wetland Functions and Values.*
23. *See* Leigh H. Frederickson, "Lowland Hardwood Wetlands: Current Status and Habitat Values for Wildlife," in *Wetland Functions and Values.*
24. Office of Technology Assessment, *Wetlands.*

25. *See* ibid., at 65.

26. Richard C. Smardon, "Visual-Cultural Values of Wetlands," in *Wetland Functions and Values.*

27. C.H. Wharton, "The Southern River Swamp."

28. Eugene P. Odum, "The Value of Wetlands: A Hierarchical Approach," in *Wetland Functions and Values;* Eugene P. Odum, "Wetlands and Their Values," *Journal of Soil and Water Conservation,* 38 (September-October, 1983): 5; Eugene P. Odum, "Wetlands As Vital Components of the Nation's Water Resources," *The Water Resources of Georgia and Adjacent Areas,* Ram Arora and Lee Gordon, eds.; Bulletin 99 Georgia Geologic Survey, Georgia Department of Natural Resources, Atlanta, Georgia, 1984.

29. Howard T. Odum, "Summary: Cypress Swamps and Their Regional Role," in *Cypress Swamps,* Katherine Carter Ewel and Howard T. Odum, eds., University of Florida Press, Gainesville, Florida, 1984.

30. Robert A. Hyatt and George A. Brook, "Ground Water Flow in the Okefenokee Swamp and Hydrologic and Nutrient Budgets for the Period August, 1981 through July, 1982."

31. Johnson et al., *An Ecological Survey of the Coastal Region of Georgia.*

32. Shaw and Fredine, *Wetlands of the United States.*

33. Ibid.

34. Ibid.

35. Ibid.

36. Ibid.

37. Hefner and Brown, "Wetland Trends in the Southeastern United States."

38. Office of Technology Assessment, *Wetlands.*

39. Tiner, *Wetlands of the United States: Current Status and Recent Trends.*

40. Ibid.

41. Ibid.

42. Ibid.

43. Office of Technology Assessment, *Wetlands.*

44. Shaw and Fredine, *Wetlands of the United States.*

45. W.M. Longley et al., "Managing Oil and Gas Activities in Coastal Environments," U.S. Fish and Wildlife Service, National Coastal Ecosystems Team, FWS/OBS-78/54, 1978.

46. Office of Technology Assessment, *Wetlands,* 120.

47. Ibid.

48. Ibid.

49. Ibid.

50. Ibid.

51. Ibid., at 122.

52. Ibid.

53. Ibid.

54. Ibid., at 123.

55. Ibid.

56. Ibid., at 124.

57. Ibid.

58. Mark T. Brown, University of Florida, National Wetland Assessment Symposium, June 19, 1985.

Chapter 3

1. Shaw and Fredine, *Wetlands of the United States.*
2. Resources Conservation Act of 1977.
3. Bruce Q. Rado and Lawrie E. Jordan, *A Case Study of the Application of Remotely-Sensed Landsat Digital Data to Georgia Natural Resource Programs.*
4. Clark et al., *Georgia, A View from Space: An Atlas of Landsat-1 Imagery.*
5. Hefner and Brown, ''Wetland Trends in the Southeastern United States.''
6. Wharton, *The Natural Environments of Georgia.*
7. Sydney A. Johnson et al., *An Ecological Survey of the Coastal Region of Georgia.*
8. Ibid.
9. Wharton, *The Natural Environments of Georgia.*
10. Eugene P. Odum, *Fundamentals of Ecology.*
11. Johnson et al., *An Ecological Survey of the Coastal Region of Georgia*; Wharton, *The Natural Environments of Georgia.*
12. Edward J. Rykiel, *The Okefenokee Swamp Watershed: Water Balance and Nutrient Budget.*
13. Hyatt and Brook, ''Ground Water Flow in the Okefenokee Swamp.''
14. William A. Pirkle and E.C. Pirkle, ''Physiographic Features and Field Relations of Trail Ridge in Northern Florida and Southeastern Georgia.''
15. Clark et al., *Georgia, A View From Space: An Atlas of Landsat-1 Imagery.*
16. David B. Hamilton, ''Plant Succession and the Influence of Disturbance in the Okefenokee Swamp.''
17. Wharton, *Natural Environments of Georgia.*
18. Ibid.
19. Robert L. Izlar, ''A History of Okefenokee Logging Operations.''
20. John R. Eadie, ''History of Okefenokee National Wildlife Refuge.''
21. Wharton, *Natural Environments of Georgia.*
22. Ibid.
23. Ibid.
24. Ibid.
25. Ibid.
26. Ibid.
27. Ibid.
28. H.T. Odum et al., ''Cypress Wetlands for Water Management, Recycling and Conservation.''
29. Wharton, *The Natural Environments of Georgia.*
30. Ibid.
31. Ibid.
32. James E. Kundell, *Ground Water Resources of Georgia.*
33. Wharton, *Natural Environments of Georgia.*
34. Richard H. Goodwin and William A. Niering, *Inland Wetlands of the United States.*
35. Tiner, *Wetlands of the United States: Current Status and Recent Trends.*
36. Hefner and Brown, ''Wetland Trends in the Southeastern United States.''
37. J. Craig Potter, presentation at National Wetland Assessment Symposium, Portland, Maine, June 16, 1985.

38. Tiner, *Wetlands of the United States: Current Status and Recent Trends.*
39. Hefner and Brown, "Wetland Trends in the Southeastern United States."
40. Office of Technology Assessment, Wetlands.
41. Ibid.

Chapter 4

1. 272 U.S. 365 (1926).
2. 277 U.S. 183 (1928).
3. Just v. Marinette County, 56 Wisc.2d 7, 201 N.W.2d 761 (1972).
4. Ibid.
5. Moskow v. Commissioner of Department of Environmental Management, 427 N.E.2d 750 (1980).
6. *E.g.* J.M. Mills, Inc. v. Murphy, 352 A.2d 661 (R.I. 1976).
7. *E.g.* Spears v. Beal, 442 N.Y.S.2d 636, 397 N.E.2d 1304 (1979).
8. *E.g.* East Haven Economic Development Commission v. Department of Environmental Protection, 36 Conn. Supp. 1, 409 A.2d 158 (1979).
9. 430 F.2d 199 (1970).
10. *See e.g.* P.F.Z. Properties, Inc. v. Train, 393 F.Supp. 1370 (D.D.C. 1975); Conservation Council of North Carolina v. Costanzo, 398 F.Supp. 653 (E.D.N.C. 1975), *aff'd,* 528 F.2d 250 (4th Circ. 1975).
11. *E.g.* American Dredging Co. v. Department of Environmental Protection, 391 A.2d 1265 (1978).
12. *E.g.* Sibson v. State of New Hampshire, 116 N.H. 644, 365 A.2d 741 (1976).
13. Potomac Sand & Gravel Co. v. Governor of Maryland, 266 Md. 358, 293 A.2d 241 (1972).
14. Thompson v. Water Resources Commission, 159 Conn. 82, 267 A.2d 434 (1970).
15. Candlestick Properties, Inc. v. San Francisco Bay Conservation and Development Commission, 11 Cal. App. 3d 557, 89 Cal.Rptr. 897 (1970).
16. Bernhard v. Caso, 19 N.Y.2d 192, 225 N.E.2d 521 (1967).
17. *In re* Board and Gales Creek Community Association, 300 N.C. 267, 266 S.E.2d 645 (N.C. 1980).
18. 399 So.2d 1374 (1981).
19. 56 Wisc.2d at 17, 201 N.W.2d at 768 (1972).
20. *See* note, "The Wetlands Controversy: A Coastal Concern Washes Inland," 52 Notre Dame Lawyer 1015, 1024; see also United States v. Carolene Products Co., 304 U.S. 144 (1938).
21. 136 N.J.Super. 436, 346 A.2d 612 (1975).
22. 266 Md. 358, 293 A.2d 241 (1972).
23. 352 A.2d 661 (R.I. 1976).
24. 95 W.Va. 377, 121 S.E. 165 (1924).
25. 40 N.J. 539, 193 A.2d 232 (1963).
26. *See* Sturdy Homes, Inc. v. Town of Redford, 30 Mich.App. 53, 186 N.W.2d 43 (1971).
27. *See* Kesselring v. Wakefield Realty Co., Inc., 306 Ky. 725, 209 S.W.2d 63 (1948).
28. *See* North Suburban Sanitary Sewer Dist. v. Water Pollution Control Commission, 281 Minn. 524, 162 N.W.2d 249 (1968).

29. Jon A. Kusler, *Our National Wetland Heritage: A Protection Guidebook.*

30. 56 Wisc.2d 7, 201 N.W.2d 761 (1972).

31. 137 N.J.Super. 179, 348 A.2d 540 (Super. Ct. App. Div. 1975).

32. 384 A.2d 610 (R.I. 1978).

33. 270 Md. 652, 313 A.2d 820 (1974).

34. Jon A. Kusler, *Our National Wetland Heritage: A Protection Guidebook.*

35. *See* Morris County Land Improvement Co. v. Parsippany-Troy Hills Township, 40 N.J. 539, 193 A.2d 232 (1963).

36. *See* Dooly v. Town Plan and Zoning Commission, 151 Conn. 304, 197 A.2d 770 (1974).

37. Just v. Marinette County, 32 Wisc.2d 608, 146 N.W.2d 577 (1966).

38. Candlestick Properties, Inc. v. San Francisco Bay Conservation and Development Commission, 11 Cal. App. 3d 557, 89 Cal.Reptr. 897 (1970).

39. 419 Pa. 504, 215 A.2d 597 (1965).

40. 657 F.2d 1184 (1981).

41. 80 U.S. 166 (1871).

42. 260 U.S. 393 (1922).

43. 369 U.S. 590 (1962).

44. Jon A. Kusler, *Our National Wetland Heritage: A Protection Guidebook.*

45. *See e.g.* Commissioner of Natural Resources v. S. Volpe & Co., Inc., 349 Mass. 104, 206 N.E.2d 666 (1965); Morris County Land Improvement Co. v. Parsippany-Troy Hills Township, 40 N.J. 539, 193 A.2d 232 (1963).

46. Jon A. Kusler, *Our National Wetland Heritage: A Protection Guidebook.*

47. *E.g.* Long v. City of Highland Park, 329 Mich. 146, 45 N.W.2d 10 (1950); City of Miami v. Romer, 73 So.2d 285 (Fla. 1954); Galt v. Cook County, 405 Ill. 396, 91 N.E.2d 395 (1950).

48. 328 U.S. 80, 83 (1946).

49. Mugler v. Kansas, 123 U.S. 623 (1887).

50. *See e.g.* Denver & Rio Grande R.R. Co. v. City and County of Denver, 250 U.S.241 (1919).

51. *See e.g.* Northwestern Fertilizing Co. v. Village of Hyde Park, 97 U.S. 659 (1878); Reinman v. City of Little Rock, 237 U.S. 171 (1915).

52. 270 Minn. 53, 133 N.W.2d 500 (1964), *cert. denied,* 382 U.S. 14 (1965).

53. 430 F.2d 199 (5th Cir. 1970), *cert. denied,* 401 U.S. 910 (1971).

54. Ibid. 430 F.2d at 203-204.

55. 266 Md. 358, 293 A.2d 241 (1972).

56. *See e.g.* Commissioner of Natural Resources v. S. Volpe & Co., Inc., 349 Mass. 104, 206 N.E.2d 666 (1965); *See* Sibson v. State of New Hampshire, 111 N.H. 305, 282 A.2d 664 (1971); Just v. Marinette County, 56 Wisc.2d 7, 201 N.W.2d 761 (1972).

57. 362 Mass. 221, 284 N.E.2d 891 (1972), *cert. denied*, 409 U.S. 1108 (1973).

58. Ibid. 284 N.E. at 899.

59. 265 A.2d 711 (Me. 1970).

60. Ibid. 265 A.2d at 717.

61. 56 Wisc.2d 7, 201 N.W.2d at 768.

62. 249 U.S. 510 (1919).

63. 393 N.E.2d 858 (Mass. 1979).

64. Jon A. Kusler, *Our National Wetland Heritage: A Protection Guidebook.*

65. 369 U.S. 590 (1962).

66. 46 N.J. 479, 218 A.2d 129 (1966), *cert. denied,* 385 U.S. 831 (1966).

67. Ibid. 218 A.2d at 137.

68. 123 U.S. 623 (1877).

69. Ibid. at 669.

70. 146 Conn. 650, 153 A.2d 822 (1959).

71. 56 Wisc.2d 7, 201 N.W.2d 761 (1972).

72. 362 Mass. 221, 284 N.E.2d 891 (1972), *cert. denied,* 409 U.S. 1108 (1973).

73. 438 U.S.104 (1978).

74. 161 N.J.Super. 504, 391 A.2d 1265 (1978).

75. 294 N.W.2d 654 (S.D. 1980).

76. Ibid. at 656.

77. *See* John S. Banta, ''Wetlands and the Taking Issue,'' *Proceedings of the National Wetland Protection Symposium,* Reston, Virginia 1977; *see generally* J. Sax, ''The Public Trust Doctrine in Natural Resource Law: Effective Judicial Intervention,'' 68 Mich. L. Rev. 471 (1970).

78. Ibid.

79. Ibid.

80. 336 A.2d 239 (N.H. 1975).

Chapter 5

1. Shaw and Fredine, *Wetlands of the United States.*

2. Ibid.

3. Jon A. Kusler, *Our National Wetland Heritage: A Protection Guidebook.*

4. Office of Technology Assessment, *Wetlands.*

5. Executive Order No. 11990, 3 CFR 121 (1977), *reprinted in* 42 USCA 4321 supp. at 191.

6. Executive Order No. 11988, 3 CFR 117 (1977), *reprinted in* 42 USCA 4321 supp. at 189.

7. Office of Technology Assessment, *Wetlands,* 74.

8. *See* 33 CFR 320.4.

9. 430 F.2d 199 (1970).

10. 33 U.S.C. 1311(a).

11. 392 F.Supp. 685 (D.D.C. 1975).

12. 40 Fed. Reg. 31320 (1975).

13. 33 CFR 209.120 (d)(2)(h) (1976).

14. *See* 123 Cong. Rec. 10426-10432 (House debate); ibid. at 26710-26729 (Senate debate).

15. CWA section 404(g)(1); 33 U.S.C. 1344(g)(1).

16. 33 CFR 323.2(c).

17. *See* U.S. v. Riverside Bayview Homes Inc., _____U.S._____(1985), No. 84-701, December 4, 1985; *reprinted in* 23 Env't. Rep. (BNA-Decisions) 1561 (December 20, 1985).

18. *See* Avoyelle's Sportmen's League v. Alexander, 715 F.2d 897 (5th Circ. 1983).

19. 33 U.S.C. 1344(f)(1); 33 U.S.C. 1344(e).

20. 14 Env't Rep. (BNA) 1787-1788 (Feb. 17, 1984); *see also* Office of Technology Assessment, *Wetlands,* 72; *see also* Thomas J. Schoenbaum, *Environmental Policy Law* (The Foundation Press, 1985) 460.

21. 33 CFR 328.

22. John Meagher, U.S. Environmental Protection Agency, presentation at National Wetland Assessment Symposium, Portland, Maine, June 18, 1985.

23. Office of Technology Assessment, *Wetlands,* 70.

24. Ibid. at 177-178.

25. Ibid. at 177-182.

26. Avoyelle's Sportsmen's League v. Alexander, 715 F.2d 897 (5th Cir. 1983).

27. Office of Technology Assessment, *Wetlands,* 141-61.

28. Ibid. at 77.

29. *See* Keith W. Harmon and Chester A. McConnel, ''The Politics of Wetland Conservation: A Wildlife View,'' *Journal of Soil and Water Conservation* 38 (March-April, 1983), 2.

30. Ibid.

31. Ibid.

32. Office of Technology Assessment, *Wetlands,* 78.

33. Jon A. Kusler, *Our National Wetland Heritage: A Protection Guidebook,* 57.

34. Office of Technology Assessment, *Wetlands,* 76.

35. Ibid.

36. Georgia Environmental Protection Division, ''Flood Hazard Workshop,'' undated.

37. R. Barrows, D. Henneberry, and S. Schwartz, ''Individual Economic Incentives, The Tax System and Wetland Protection Policy: A Study of Returns to Wetlands Drainage in Southeastern Wisconsin,'' American Society of Agricultural Engineers, summer meeting, 1982, p. 26.

38. Office of Technology Assessment, *Wetlands,* 80.

39. 16 USCA Section 669 (1974 and supp. 1980).

40. Joe Kurz, Game and Fish Division of the Georgia Department of Natural Resources, personal communication.

41. 16 USCA Section 777 (1974 and supp. 1980).

42. Jon A. Kusler, *Our National Wetland Heritage: A Protection Guidebook,* 104.

43. Tim Hess, Game and Fish Division of the Georgia Department of Natural Resources, personal communication.

44. Ibid.

45. Office of Technology Assessment, *Wetlands,* 76.

46. Ibid., at 77.

47. Ibid.

48. *See* Jon A. Kusler, *Our National Wetland Heritage: A Protection Guidebook,* 65.

49. Ibid.; Maine has recently adopted an inland wetland statute.

50. This analysis is adapted from Jon A. Kusler, *Our National Wetland Heritage: A Protection Guidebook.*

51. Georgia Code, Section 12-5-285(f).

52. *See* N.H. REV. STAT. ANN. ch. 483-A.

53. *See* R.I. Gen. Laws sections 2-1-8 through 2-1-25.

54. *See* CONN. GEN. STAT. sections 22a-36 through 22a-45.

55. *See* FLA. STAT. ANN. section 403.91 et seq.

56. *See* ME. REV. STAT. tit. 12, sections 7776-7780.

57. *See* ME. REV. STAT. tit. 38, sections 386-396.

58. *See* Maine Legislative Service 1985, ch. 485.

59. *See* Mass. Gen. Laws ch. 131, section 40.

60. *See* Mass. Gen. Laws ch. 131, section 40-A.

61. *See* Mich. Compiled Laws Ann. sections 281.702 et seq.

62. *See* MINN. STAT. ch. 105.37 through 105.391.

63. *See* N.Y. Envir. Conserv. Law art. 24.

64. Office of Technology Assessment, *Wetlands,* 81-83.

65. 16 U.S.C. Section 1456(c) (1976 and supp. 1980).

66. Office of Technology Assessment, *Wetlands,* 83.

67. Ibid.

68. Jon A. Kusler, *Our National Wetland Heritage: A Protection Guidebook.*

69. Georgia Department of Revenue, ''Report Reflecting the Impact of Preferential Assessment of Property Devoted to Agricultural Purposes for 1984,'' January, 1985.

70. Nancy E. Duhnkrack, ''Senate Bill 397: A New Approach to Riparian Area Protection in Oregon.''

71. Ibid.

72. Ibid.

73. Jon A. Kusler, *Our National Wetland Heritage: A Protection Guidebook,* 71.

74. Ibid.

75. Ibid.

Chapter 6

1. Eugene P. Odum, Institute of Ecology, University of Georgia, personal communication.

2. C.H. Wharton, ''The Southern River Swamp.''

3. Fred Marland, Coastal Division, Georgia Department of Natural Resources, personal communication.

4. National Wetland Assessment Symposium, Portland, Maine, June 16-19, 1985.

5. Carl Dierker, Office of the Massachusetts Attorney General, presentation at the National Wetland Assessment Symposium, June 18, 1985.

6. Patricia Riexinger, New York State Department of Environmental Conservation, presentation at National Wetland Assessment Symposium, June 19, 1985.

7. Scott Hausmann, Wisconsin Dept. of Natural Resources, presentation at National Wetland Assessment Symposium, June 19, 1985.

8. Carl Pagel, Vermont Dept. of Water Resources, presentation at National Wetland Assessment Symposium, June 19, 1985.

9. Khervin Smith, Pennsylvania Dept. Natural Resources, presentation at National Wetland Assessment Symposium, June 19, 1985

10. James E. Kundell, et al., *Prime Farmland in Georgia.*

11. John Bozeman, Coastal Division, Georgia Dept. of Natural Resources, personal communication.

12. John Mixon, Director, Georgia Forestry Commission, personal communication.

References

Banta, John S. "Wetlands and the Taking Issue," *Proceedings of the National Wetland Protection Symposium,* U.S. Fish and Wildlife Service, Washington, D.C., 1977.

Barrows, R., D. Henneberry and S. Schwartz. "Individual Economic Incentives, the Tax System, and Wetland Protection Policy: A Study of Returns to Wetlands Drainage in Southeastern Wisconsin," American Society of Agricultural Engineers, Summer Meeting, 1982.

Brown, M.T. and E.M. Starnes. *A Wetland Study of Seminole County.* Center for Wetlands, University of Florida, Gainesville, Florida, 1983.

Clark, William Z., Jr., Arnold C. Zisa, and Richard C. Jones. *Georgia, A View from Space: An Atlas of Landsat-1 Imagery.* Georgia Department of Natural Resources, Atlanta, Georgia, 1976.

Cowardin, L.M., V. Carter, F.C. Golet, and E.T. LaRoe. *Classification of Wetlands and Deepwater Habitats of the United States.* U.S. Department of Interior, Fish and Wildlife Service, Washington, D.C., 1979.

Duhnkrack, Nancy E. "Senate Bill 397: A New Approach to Riparian Area Protection in Oregon," in *California Riparian Systems.* Richard E. Warner and Kathleen M. Hendrix, eds. University of California, Berkeley, California, 1984.

Eadie, John R. "History of Okefenokee National Wildlife Refuge," in *The Okefenokee Swamp.* A.D. Cohen, D.J. Casagrande, M.J. Andrejko, and G.R. Best, eds. Wetland Surveys, Los Alamos, New Mexico, 1984.

Ewel, Katherine Carter, and Howard T. Odum, eds. *Cypress Swamp,* University of Florida Press, Gainesville, Florida, 1984.

Georgia Department of Natural Resources. *Georgia Statewide Landsat Classification Statistics by County.* In cooperation with Georgia Institute of Technology, Atlanta, Georgia, 1979.

Georgia Department of Revenue. *Department of Revenue's Report Reflecting the Impact of Preferential Assessment of Property Devoted to Agricultural Purposes for 1984.* Atlanta, Georgia, January, 1985.

Goodwin, Richard H. and William A. Niering. *Inland Wetlands of the United States.* U.S. Department of the Interior, National Park Service, Washington, D.C., 1975.

Hamilton, David B. "Plant Succession and the Influence of Disturbance in the Okefenokee Swamp," *The Okefenokee Swamp.* A.D. Cohen, D.J. Casagrande, M.J. Andrejko, G.R. Best, eds. Wetland Surveys, Los Alamos, New Mexico, 1984.

Harmon, Keith W. and Chester A. McConnel. "The Politics of Wetland Conservation: A Wildlife View," *Journal of Soil and Water Conservation,* 38:2, March-April, 1983.

Hefner, John M. and James D. Brown. "Wetland Trends in the Southeastern United States." Fifth Annual Meeting of the Society of Wetland Scientists, San Francisco, California, 1984.

Hyatt, Robert A. and George A. Brook. "Ground Water Flow in the Okefenokee Swamp and Hydrologic and Nutrient Budgets for the Period August, 1981 through July, 1982," in *The Okefenokee Swamp.* A.D. Cohen, D.J. Casagrande, M.J. Andrejko, and G.R. Best, eds. Wetland Surveys, Los Alamos, New Mexico, 1984.

Izlar, Robert L. "A History of Okefenokee Logging Operations," in *The Okefenokee Swamp.* A.D. Cohen, D.J. Casagrande, M.J. Andrejko, and G.R. Best, eds. Wetland Surveys, Los Alamos, New Mexico, 1984.

Johnson, A. Sydney, Hilburn O. Hillestad, Sheryl Fanning Shanholtzer, and G. Frederick Shanholtzer. *An Ecological Survey of the Coastal Region of Georgia.* Scientific Monograph Series, U.S. Department of Interior, National Park Service, Washington, D.C., 1974.

Kundell, James E. *Ground Water Resources of Georgia.* Institute of Government, University of Georgia, Athens, Georgia, 1978.

Kundell, James E., Fred C. White, and Johnnie Graham. *Prime Farmland in Georgia.* Institute of Government, University of Georgia, Athens, Georgia, 1982.

Kusler, Jon A. *Our National Wetland Heritage: A Protection Guidebook.* Environmental Law Institute, Washington, D.C., 1983.

Odum, Eugene P. *Fundamentals of Ecology.* Saunders, Philadelphia, Pennsylvania, 1959.

_____. ''The Value of Wetlands: A Hierarchical Approach,'' in *Wetland Functions and Values: The State of Our Understanding.* Phillip Greeson, John R. Clark, and Judith E. Clark, eds. Proceedings of the National Symposium on Wetlands, American Waters Resource Association, Minneapolis, Minnesota, 1979.

_____. ''Wetlands and Their Values. *Journal of Soil and Water Conservation* 38 (September-October 1983), 5.

_____. ''Wetlands As Vital Components of the Nation's Water Resources,'' in *The Water Resources of Georgia and Adjacent Areas.* Ram Arora and Lee Gordon, eds.; Bulletin 99, Georgia Geologic Survey, Georgia Department of Natural Resources, Atlanta, Georgia, 1984.

Odum, Howard T. et al. *Cypress Wetlands for Water Management, Recycling, and Conservation.* Center for Wetlands, University of Florida, Gainesville, Florida, 1984.

Office of Technology Assessment. *Wetlands: Their Use and Regulation.* United States Congress, Washington, D.C., 1984.

Pirkle, William A. and E.C. Pirkle. ''Physiographic Features and Field Relations of Trail Ridge in Northern Florida and Southeastern Georgia,'' in *The Okefenokee Swamp.* A.D. Cohen, D.J. Casagrande, M.J. Andrejko, and G.R. Best, eds. Wetland Surveys, Los Alamos, New Mexico, 1984.

Rado, Bruce Q. and Lawrie E. Jordan, III. *A Case Study of the Application of Remotely-Sensed Landsat Digital Data to Georgia Natural Resource Programs. Final Report.* Georgia Department of Natural Resources, Atlanta, Georgia, 1977.

Rykiel, Edward J., Jr. *The Okefenokee Swamp Watershed: Water Balance and Nutrient Budget.* University of Georgia, Athens, Georgia, 1977.

Shaw, Samuel P. and C. Gordon Fredine. *Wetlands of the United States: Their Extent and Their Value to Waterfowl and Other Wildlife.* Circular 39. U.S. Department of the Interior, Fish and Wildlife Service, Washington, D.C., 1956.

Schoenbaum, Thomas J. *Environmental Policy Law.* The Foundation Press, Inc., Mineola, New York, 1985.

Tiner, Ralph W., Jr. *Wetlands of the United States: Current Status and Recent Trends.* U.S. Department of the Interior, Fish and Wildlife Service, Washington, D.C., 1984.

Wharton, Charles H. *The Southern River Swamp—A Multiple Use Environment.* Bureau of Business and Economic Research, School of Business Administration, Georgia State University, Atlanta, Georgia, 1970.

Wharton, Charles H. *The Natural Environments of Georgia.* Georgia Department of Natural Resources, Atlanta, Georgia, 1978.

Appendix: Acres of Wetlands, by County

County	Acres of Forested Wetlands	County	Acres of Forested Wetlands
1 Ware	126303	40 Wheeler	22893
2 Charlton	110747	41 Liberty	22738
3 Burke	77374	42 Cook	22722
4 Clinch	74726	43 Lanier	22360
5 Wayne	59864	44 Richmond	22360
6 Thomas	57417	45 Jeff Davis	21450
7 Screven	56465	46 Pierce	20933
8 Brooks	56185	47 Camden	20611
9 Long	53275	48 Houston	19429
10 Lowndes	51398	49 Chatham	18763
11 Grady	49574	50 Ben Hill	18414
12 Jefferson	41968	51 Columbia	18133
13 Brantley	40797	52 Tift	17822
14 Dougherty	40224	53 Montgomery	17614
15 Sumter	40096	54 Crisp	16844
16 Tattnall	39645	55 Bryan	16544
17 Dodge	38593	56 Turner	15622
18 Berrien	37902	57 Twiggs	14780.7
19 Telfair	37792	58 Glynn	14556.7
20 Colquitt	37344	59 Early	14147.1
21 Lee	35787	60 McIntosh	14019.1
22 Worth	35563	61 Treutlen	13817.5
23 Coffee	34983	62 Bacon	13790.3
24 Appling	33998	63 Baker	13294.3
25 Echols	33701	64 Bibb	13217.5
26 Wilcox	31688	65 Calhoun	12647.9
27 Dooly	31038	66 Evans	11734.3
28 Pulaski	30552	67 Macon	11395.1
29 Bulloch	29645	68 Candler	9614.3
30 Laurens	28398	69 Decatur	9180.8
31 Effingham	28245	70 Terrell	8971.1
32 Wilkinson	25937	71 Johnson	8745.5
33 Irwin	25718	72 Troup	8511.9
34 Emanuel	25446	73 Miller	8383.9
35 Mitchell	25141	74 Seminole	7985.6
36 Jenkins	25129	75 Crawford	7516.8
37 Washington	24137	76 Taylor	6948.8
38 Atkinson	23886	77 Bleckley	6577.6
39 Toombs	23230	78 Coweta	6574.4

County	Acres of Forested Wetlands	County	Acres of Forested Wetlands
79 Meriwether	6489.6	120 Rockdale	1755.2
80 Randolph	6366.4	121 Schley	1673.6
81 Baldwin	6083.2	122 Haralson	1427.2
82 Walton	5892.8	123 DeKalb	596.8
83 Stewart	5840.0	124 Banks	0.0
84 Putnam	5652.8	125 Barrow	0.0
85 Harris	5235.2	126 Bartow	0.0
86 Fayette	5204.8	127 Catoosa	0.0
87 Morgan	4508.8	128 Chattooga	0.0
88 Jasper	4404.8	129 Cherokee	0.0
89 Hancock	4337.6	130 Clarke	0.0
90 Newton	4307.2	131 Cobb	0.0
91 Chattahoochee	4296.0	132 Dade	0.0
92 Webster	4203.2	133 Dawson	0.0
93 McDuffie	3840.0	134 Elbert	0.0
94 Carroll	3534.4	135 Fannin	0.0
95 Pike	3520.0	136 Floyd	0.0
96 Glascock	3476.8	137 Forsyth	0.0
97 Greene	3441.6	138 Franklin	0.0
98 Spalding	3412.8	139 Gilmer	0.0
99 Wilkes	3361.6	140 Gordon	0.0
100 Muscogee	3209.6	141 Gwinnett	0.0
101 Henry	3182.4	142 Habersham	0.0
102 Upson	3148.8	143 Hall	0.0
103 Fulton	3099.2	144 Hart	0.0
104 Talbot	2929.6	145 Jackson	0.0
105 Quitman	2840.0	146 Lincoln	0.0
106 Clayton	2763.2	147 Lumpkin	0.0
107 Jones	2665.6	148 Madison	0.0
108 Warren	2528.0	149 Murray	0.0
109 Taliaferro	2436.8	150 Paulding	0.0
110 Monroe	2382.4	151 Pickens	0.0
111 Heard	2332.8	152 Polk	0.0
112 Marion	2259.2	153 Rabun	0.0
113 Clay	2176.0	154 Stephens	0.0
114 Douglas	2089.6	155 Towns	0.0
115 Lamar	1952.2	156 Union	0.0
116 Butts	1944.0	157 Walker	0.0
117 Peach	1843.2	158 White	0.0
118 Oconee	1822.4	159 Whitfield	0.0
119 Oglethorpe	1817.6		

County	Acres of Freshwater Wetlands	County	Acres of Freshwater Wetlands
1 Ware	126303	46 Wheeler	22893
2 Charlton	110747	47 Cook	22722
3 Burke	77374	48 Lanier	22360
4 Clinch	74726	49 Richmond	22360
5 Wayne	59864	50 Jeff Davis	21450
6 Thomas	57417	51 Pierce	20933
7 Screven	56465	52 Houston	19429
8 Brooks	56185	53 Ben Hill	18414
9 Long	53275	54 Columbia	18133
10 Lowndes	51398	55 Tift	17822
11 Grady	49574	56 Montgomery	17614
12 Jefferson	41968	57 Crisp	16843.9
13 Brantley	40797	58 Turner	15622.3
14 Dougherty	40224	59 Twiggs	14780.7
15 Sumter	40096	60 Early	14147.1
16 Tattnall	39645	61 Treutlen	13817.5
17 Dodge	38593	62 Bacon	13790.3
18 Berrien	37902	63 Baker	13294.3
19 Telfair	37792	64 Bibb	13217.5
20 Colquitt	37344	65 Calhoun	12647.9
21 Lee	35787	66 Evans	11734.3
22 Worth	35563	67 Macon	11395.1
23 Coffee	34982	68 Candler	9614.3
24 Liberty	34333	69 Decatur	9180.8
25 Appling	33998	70 Terrell	8971.1
26 Echols	33701	71 Johnson	8745.5
27 Wilcox	31688	72 Troup	8511.9
28 Dooly	31038	73 Miller	8383.9
29 Chatham	31027	74 Seminole	7985.6
30 Camden	30861	75 Crawford	7516.8
31 Pulaski	30552	76 Taylor	6948.8
32 Bulloch	29645	77 Bleckley	6577.6
33 Laurens	28398	78 Coweta	6574.4
34 Effingham	28245	79 Meriwether	6489.6
35 Bryan	26257	80 Randolph	6366.4
36 Wilkinson	25937	81 Baldwin	6083.2
37 Irwin	25718	82 Walton	5892.8
38 Emanuel	25446	83 Stewart	5840.0
39 McIntosh	25221	84 Putnam	5652.8
40 Mitchell	25141	85 Harris	5235.2
41 Jenkins	25129	86 Fayette	5204.8
42 Washington	24137	87 Morgan	4508.8
43 Glynn	23951	88 Jasper	4404.8
44 Atkinson	23886	89 Hancock	4337.6
45 Toombs	23230	90 Newton	4307.2

County	Acres of Freshwater Wetlands	County	Acres of Freshwater Wetlands
91 Chattahoochee	4296.0	126 Bartow	0.0
92 Webster	4203.2	127 Catoosa	0.0
93 McDuffie	3840.0	128 Chattooga	0.0
94 Carroll	3534.4	129 Cherokee	0.0
95 Pike	3520.0	130 Clarke	0.0
96 Glascock	3476.8	131 Cobb	0.0
97 Greene	3441.6	132 Dade	0.0
98 Spalding	3412.8	133 Dawson	0.0
99 Wilkes	3361.6	134 Elbert	0.0
100 Muscogee	3209.6	135 Fannin	0.0
101 Henry	3182.4	136 Floyd	0.0
102 Upson	3148.8	137 Forsyth	0.0
103 Fulton	3099.2	138 Franklin	0.0
104 Talbot	2929.6	139 Gilmer	0.0
105 Quitman	2840.0	140 Gordon	0.0
106 Clayton	2763.2	141 Gwinnett	0.0
107 Jones	2665.6	142 Habersham	0.0
108 Warren	2528.0	143 Hall	0.0
109 Taliaferro	2436.8	144 Hart	0.0
110 Monroe	2382.4	145 Jackson	0.0
111 Heard	2332.8	146 Lincoln	0.0
112 Marion	2259.2	147 Lumpkin	0.0
113 Clay	2176.0	148 Madison	0.0
114 Douglas	2089.6	149 Murray	0.0
115 Lamar	1952.2	150 Paulding	0.0
116 Butts	1944.0	151 Pickens	0.0
117 Peach	1843.2	152 Polk	0.0
118 Oconee	1822.4	153 Rabun	0.0
118 Oglethorpe	1817.6	154 Stephens	0.0
120 Rockdale	1755.2	155 Towns	0.0
121 Schley	1673.6	156 Union	0.0
122 Haralson	1427.2	157 Walker	0.0
123 DeKalb	596.8	158 White	0.0
124 Banks	0.0	159 Whitfield	0.0
125 Barrow	0.0		

County	Acres of Total Wetlands	County	Acres of Total Wetlands
1 Chatham	149108	46 Wheeler	22893
2 McIntosh	142988	47 Cook	22722
3 Camden	132188	48 Lanier	22360
4 Ware	126303	49 Richmond	22360
5 Glynn	120218	50 Jeff Davis	21450
6 Liberty	113675	51 Pierce	20933
7 Charlton	110747	52 Houston	19429
8 Burkes	77374	53 Ben Hill	18414
9 Bryan	75976	54 Columbia	18133
10 Clinchs	74726	55 Tift	17822
11 Wayne	59864	56 Montgomery	17614
12 Thomas	57417	57 Crisp	16843.9
13 Screven	56465	58 Turner	15622.3
14 Brooks	56185	59 Twiggs	14780.7
15 Long	53275	60 Early	14147.1
16 Lowndes	51398	61 Treutlen	13817.5
17 Grady	49574	62 Bacon	13790.3
18 Jefferson	41968	63 Baker	13294.3
19 Brantley	40797	64 Bibb	13217.5
20 Dougherty	40224	65 Calhoun	12647.9
21 Sumter	40096	66 Evans	11734.3
22 Tattnall	39645	67 Macon	11395.1
23 Dodge	38593	68 Candler	9614.3
24 Berrien	37902	69 Decatur	9180.8
25 Telfair	37792	70 Terrell	8971.1
26 Colquitt	37344	71 Johnson	8745.5
27 Lee	35787	72 Troup	8511.9
28 Worth	35563	73 Miller	8383.9
29 Coffee	34982	74 Seminole	7985.6
30 Appling	33998	75 Crawford	7516.8
31 Echols	33701	76 Taylor	6948.8
32 Wilcox	31688	77 Bleckley	6577.6
33 Dooly	31038	78 Coweta	6574.4
34 Pulaski	30552	79 Meriwether	6489.6
35 Bulloch	29645	80 Randolph	6366.4
36 Laurens	28398	81 Baldwin	6083.2
37 Effingham	28245	82 Walton	5892.8
38 Wilkinson	25937	83 Stewart	5840.0
39 Irwin	25718	84 Putnam	5652.8
40 Emanuel	25446	85 Harris	5235.2
41 Mitchell	25141	86 Fayette	5204.8
42 Jenkins	25129	87 Morgan	4508.8
43 Washington	24137	88 Jasper	4404.8
44 Atkinson	22886	89 Hancock	4337.6
45 Toombs	23230	90 Newton	4307.2

County	Acres of Total Wetlands	County	Acres of Total Wetlands
91 Chattahoochee	4296.0	126 Bartow	0.0
92 Webster	4203.2	127 Catoosa	0.0
93 McDuffie	3840.0	128 Chattooga	0.0
94 Carroll	3534.4	129 Cherokee	0.0
95 Pike	3520.0	130 Clarke	0.0
96 Glascock	3476.8	131 Cobb	0.0
97 Greene	3441.6	132 Dade	0.0
98 Spalding	3412.8	133 Dawson	0.0
99 Wilkes	3361.6	134 Elbert	0.0
100 Muscogee	3209.6	135 Fannin	0.0
101 Henry	3182.4	136 Floyd	0.0
102 Upson	3148.8	137 Forsyth	0.0
103 Fulton	3099.2	138 Franklin	0.0
104 Talbot	2929.6	139 Gilmer	0.0
105 Quitman	2840.0	140 Gordon	0.0
106 Clayton	2763.2	141 Gwinnett	0.0
107 Jones	2665.6	142 Habersham	0.0
108 Warren	2528.0	143 Hall	0.0
109 Taliaferro	2436.8	144 Hart	0.0
110 Monroe	2382.4	145 Jackson	0.0
111 Heard	2332.8	146 Lincoln	0.0
112 Marion	2259.2	147 Lumpkin	0.0
113 Clay	2176.0	148 Madison	0.0
114 Douglas	2089.6	149 Murray	0.0
115 Lamar	1952.2	150 Paulding	0.0
116 Butts	1944.0	151 Pickens	0.0
117 Peach	1843.2	152 Polk	0.0
118 Oconee	1822.4	153 Rabun	0.0
118 Oglethorpe	1817.6	154 Stephens	0.0
120 Rockdale	1755.2	155 Towns	0.0
121 Schley	1673.6	156 Union	0.0
122 Haralson	1427.2	157 Walker	0.0
123 DeKalb	596.8	158 White	0.0
124 Banks	0.0	159 Whitfield	0.0
125 Barrow	0.0		